His Intent

The Father's Passion for His Son's Church

By Geoff Vaine

Kingdom Publishers

His Intent

Copyright© Geoff Vaine

All rights reserved. No part of this book may be reproduced in any form by photocopying or any electronic or mechanical means, including information storage or retrieval systems, without permission in writing from both the copyright owner and the publisher of the book. The right of Geoff Vaine to be identified as the author of this work has been asserted by him in accordance with the Copyright, Designs and Patents Act 1988 and any subsequent amendments thereto.
A catalogue record for this book is available from the British Library.
All Scripture quotations unless otherwise stated have been taken from the New International Version of the Bible

ISBN: 978-1-7398763-0-2

1st Edition by Kingdom Publishers, London, UK.

You can purchase copies of this book from any leading bookstore or email contact@kingdompublishers.co.uk

Table of Contents

Acknowledgments	9
Preface	11
Introduction to Part 1	**15**
Chapter 1: The Bride	17
Chapter 2: A Great Harvest (1) – The Prominence of the Church	23
Chapter 3: A Great Harvest (2) – The Place for Revival	31
Chapter 4: A Wedding Planned	43
Chapter 5: What is the Church?	51
Chapter 6: The Church in Practice	59
Chapter 7: The Church as a Body	67
Chapter 8: The Work of the Holy Spirit	73
Chapter 9: Breadboard, Breadcrumbs or Fresh Bread?	83
Chapter 10: Grasping the Horns of the Altar	93
Chapter 11: The Design Brief	101
Chapter 12: The Church is a Building Site!	113
Chapter 13: Looking Back to Move Forward	119
Introduction to Part 2	**129**
Chapter 14: His Intent	131
Chapter 15: Through the Church	135
Chapter 16: The Manifold Wisdom of God	141
Chapter 17: Rulers and Authorities	150
Chapter 18: Wrapping Things Up	153

His Intent

God's intent was that now, through the church, the manifold wisdom of God might be made known to the rulers and authorities in the heavenly realms
Ephesians 3:10

Acknowledgements

My grateful thanks to Ros, Derek and Janet who laboured over many months, painstakingly working through the manuscripts of each chapter, editing and making valuable suggestions for additions and deletions.

Thank you also to Andrew from Kingdom Publishers for his erstwhile work in the final editing process.

I am also indebted to Kingdom Publishers for agreeing to take on this publication and for the helpful comments and suggestions they have made in order to get *His Intent* into print.

Preface

God wanted this book to be written, through the leading of the Holy Spirit. This statement may seem, to some, to be rather bold, presumptuous or bordering on the arrogant. However, as I set out writing the drafts, I became very much aware that this wasn't going to be a simple exposition on Ephesians 3:10, but as I went along, I felt God prompting me with the occasional word or phrase that would set me off on a new tack and the words poured out through the keyboard onto computer screen!

Like many who pick up this book, I had read the book of Ephesians countless times. I had heard any number of sermons relating to this letter of the apostle Paul. But as so often happens when reading familiar bible passages, as I read the well-known Chapter 3, something really gripped me about the text, especially verse 10 and in particular the phrase *'through the church'*

I knew God was saying something to me but what exactly I didn't really know. It was only as I started to put finger to keyboard that a way forward began to develop.

The picture of the wedding scene came to mind first - a sort of look forward to the wonderful culmination of God's plan for His church and this seemed to set the background for the rest of this book.

So, although this book is a form of study into verse 10 it is so much more and I pray the Holy Spirit speaks to you in reading it through. Not everyone will agree with what I have written. There will be some who will argue from scripture how my writing isn't the case. However, I can only write that which I believe God has given me and pray that He will reveal to you His purpose for His great church.

Geoff Vaine
February 2023

PART 1 – THE CHURCH

I will build My church .... Matthew 16:18

Introduction to Part 1

In writing this book based on a single verse of scripture, one might have thought it would have started with the actual verse and developed from there and yes, if I had sat down and planned it out, that might well have been the starting point. However, as I have said in the Preface, I felt the Holy Spirit's leading in a different direction, and so, in this first part, I have focussed on the church itself.

The Church, as we will see, is the vehicle through which the work of Jesus, both in His teaching and example in daily living, as well as His sanctifying work through the Cross and Resurrection, is made known to the world in which it is situated.

It is always a profound mystery why God chooses people such as ourselves to achieve this desire, as we can always point to others whom we consider better than ourselves, and we would be correct in contemplating this, as scripture cautions us:

> "Do not think of yourself more highly than you ought, but rather think of yourself with sober judgment, in accordance with the faith God has distributed to each of you."
> (Romans 12:3)

However, Paul also reveals something of God's reasoning behind this, when he says:

> "Brothers and sisters, think of what you were when you were called. Not many of you were wise by human standards; not many were influential; not many were of noble birth. But God chose the foolish things of the world to shame the wise; God chose the weak things of the world to shame the strong. God chose the lowly things of this world and the despised things - and the things that are not - to nullify the things that are, so that no one may boast before Him." (1 Corinthians 1:26-29)

I haven't covered every aspect of the church in Part 1 – there are already many books written that more than adequately cover the topic far better than I can, but it does give an overview which helps to apply the text which is studied in Part II.

Chapter One

The Bride

The car winds its way through the town in the early afternoon traffic. People stop to look at the car and catch a glimpse of its occupants, for there is no mistaking the white ribbons on the bonnet and the door handles that mark it out as a wedding car. Women point out to their children the bride dressed in white sitting next to her proud father, seeing if they might know them and wondering where the wedding is taking place.

Meanwhile, in the church the guests have arrived. Many have travelled great distances to be here. This is one wedding they definitely do not want to miss! It's a once in a life time opportunity and they have made sure they are going to be there.

The church looks resplendent, decked out with flowers, skilfully arranged in enormous bouquets in ornate vases. Pastel coloured drapes have been carefully placed to show off the flowers and surroundings, and sunlight coming through the stained-glass windows illuminates beautifully the vibrant colours of both.

The gathered congregation whisper in hushed tones, as they expectantly await the arrival of the bride. What will her dress look like? It has been a closely guarded secret, with only the bride's mother and seamstress 'in the know'. How many bridesmaids will there be? Will there be cute little pageboys they wonder?

The groom looks nervous, as would be expected. Trying to make a joke with his best man to break the tension, but not really succeeding, He has waited a long time for this day and now it is here. His intended, the woman he has wooed over time will, today, be his wife and they will live happily for the rest of their lives.

The Bride

There is movement at the back of the church. Some look round to see if this is the moment they were waiting for. The organist awaits the signal to change his music to the well-known entrance music. The bride's mother arrives, accompanied to her place by the chief usher.

Further movement at the entrance door. The signal is given to the organist, who skilfully changes key, and then a great chord booms out as Mendelssohn's wedding march begins and they know the bride has arrived and is about to make her slow, graceful way down the aisle. The congregation stand, the groom and best man take their places. People peer round trying to catch a first glimpse of the bride as she walks carefully down the aisle, with her proud father by her side.

The bridesmaids follow, honoured to be attending this delightful friend and relative, the little ones not quite knowing what is happening but recognising it is a very special occasion. The pageboys are feeling very self-conscious in their outfits, trying not to look too pleased about their role, lest their friends find out and tease them about it later at school.

The bride, looking radiant, glances occasionally left and right catching the eye of one or two as she makes her way gracefully to the front of the church, simply bursting with love and joy on her special day. Soon she will be joined with the man of her dreams.

This is a well-known scene with which we are probably familiar, played out in hundreds of churches up and down the country on many weekends – especially during the summer months. The day has taken months and months of planning, - such is the demand for churches and reception venues, they can get booked up two years or more in advance.

This day is the culmination of a romance that has blossomed over time, perhaps even from schooldays. Friends and relatives have watched as the friendship turned to love and devotion, then the announcement of an engagement. Too soon, the wheels of the great wedding machinery have sprung into action, and a card dropped through the door one morning, *"Save the day"* it announced, teasing you with the scarcest of information, knowing what it was about, but pleased to be included and forewarned anyway.

The Church as a Bride

The Church is portrayed in the bible as a Bride – the Bride of Christ. Jesus taught His followers about the kingdom of God many times. On one occasion, He began to teach them about a wedding banquet:

> The kingdom of heaven is like a king who prepared a wedding banquet for his son. (Matthew 22:2)

Here, Jesus begins to describe to His listeners an event, that we now know as the final gathering of believers in Jesus, which we read of in the book of Revelation:

> Let us rejoice and be glad
>   and give Him glory!
> For the wedding of the Lamb has come,
>   and His bride has made herself ready.
> Fine linen, bright and clean,
>   was given her to wear."
>
> (Fine linen stands for the righteous acts of God's holy people.)
>
> Then the angel said to me, "Write this: Blessed are those who are invited to the wedding supper of the Lamb!" And he added, "These are the true words of God." (Revelation 19:7-9)

The apostle, Paul, when writing to the church in Ephesus, gives instruction to husbands and wives for conduct within marriage. When speaking to the husbands he tells them:

> Husbands, love your wives, just as Christ loved the church and gave Himself up for her to make her holy, cleansing her by the washing with water through the word, and to present her to Himself as a radiant church, without stain or wrinkle or any other blemish, but holy and blameless. (Ephesians 5:25-27)

Paul gives further emphasis that he is referring to the relationship between Jesus and His church:

> "For this reason, a man will leave his father and mother and be united to his wife, and the two will become one flesh." This is a profound mystery—but I am talking about Christ and the church. (Ephesians 5:31-32)

The reader will readily identify this image with a bride on her wedding day. The bride is indeed radiant, she gets heads turning and is the focus of attention – even whilst in the car travelling to her wedding.

Jesus is in love with the church – passionately in love with her! This love motivates His actions towards her with tenderness and care that, as we shall see in later chapters, His hope and expectancy is that the church will be triumphant and glorious because He will ensure that it happens.

His passion for the church knows no ends. He will continue to woo her and prepare her for the wedding that will surely come.

Note the use of Paul's words in Ephesians 5 above – *cleansing, make her holy, presenting her* – all these indicate a period of preparation in readiness for the final gathering – the wedding of the Lamb of God. The church has always been in this phase since it burst on the scene at Pentecost. Jesus is patient, He will not hurry this preparation time. Whilst it is true Jesus doesn't know how long He has to prepare the church - only God the Father knows this, (Matthew 24:36) Jesus will not be caught out still waiting for the bride to be ready. There will be a coming together of God the Father, His Son Jesus, and the Holy Spirit, so that the timing will be perfectly aligned as we have seen in Revelation 19:7-9.

Jesus' bride has '*made herself ready*' (v7) and indicates that a time will come when the church knows how to make the final preparations. The Holy Spirit will move upon the church in such a way that in the last few days, months or years – we do not know, there will be a sense, as we say, 'this is it'. In the same way that a bride makes her final preparations on the morning of her wedding, so also the church will come to that point in its life, when there is a hastening of the wedding preparations.

A Sense of Expectancy

Before Jesus came to earth there had been no prophetic activity for nearly 400 years, but prior to His birth, people just had a 'sense' that something was about to happen.

> Now there was a man in Jerusalem called Simeon, who was righteous and devout. He was waiting for the consolation of Israel, and the Holy Spirit was on him. It had been revealed to him by the Holy Spirit that he would not die before he had seen the Lord's Messiah. (Luke 2:25-26)

Simeon was waiting expectantly for the Messiah to appear because of a witness within him from the Holy Spirit. In the same way, I believe the church will know when 'The Wedding' is getting close. As I have already said, we will not know when the exact time will come, but I sincerely believe we will have that sense of expectancy and the Bride will be led in to making her final preparations - whatever form they may take.

Jesus gave a powerful example to His disciples when they asked Him about these days. He spoke to them about ten virgins awaiting the arrival of the bridegroom (Matthew 25:1-13). Five of them are described as wise, being well prepared for the wait, whilst the other five are portrayed as foolish, thinking only of the immediate time period. Jesus ends the parable with this warning:

> "Therefore, keep watch, because you do not know the day or the hour". (Matthew 25:13)

Dr Martyn Lloyd Jones, the medical doctor turned church minister who led Westminster Chapel in London for over 30 years, said this about the church:

> When the church is absolutely different from the world, she invariably attracts it. It is then that the world is made to listen to her message, though it may hate it at first.[1]

---

[1] Martyn Lloyd Jones – (Various sources)

As with the bride in our earlier illustration, heads turn as she travels in her wedding car through a town or city, so Dr Lloyd Jones says here, *'the church will attract people, when she is different from the world'*.

As we've looked at this analogy of the church as a bride, I've tried to show the reader something of what the church has in store for it in the future and it is this church that God wants to use – and is indeed using now, to make known His multi-faceted, manifold wisdom, to the world and the heavenly realms.

In succeeding chapters in Part 1, we examine what the church is and in Part II unpack the text in Ephesians 3:10. I hope you will recognise how God is unequivocally committed to using the church to bring about His plans and purposes.

Chapter Two

A Great Harvest (1)
The Prominence of the Church

"When the church is absolutely different from the world, she invariably attracts it. It is then that the world is made to listen to her message, though it may hate it at first."
(Dr Martyn Lloyd Jones)

The early church could not be accused of hiding, being inconspicuous, unknown or obscure. In one short day the believers in Jesus went from 120 to 3,000. The church literally exploded onto the scene. From there onwards, no one could ignore what God was doing with the new 'way' as it was termed.

New believers were added *daily* and their number rapidly expanded to 5,000+ in a few weeks. On numerous occasions in the book of Acts, Dr Luke recorded people being added to their number. Even when two of them lied about the amount of money they got for selling a field and died as a result of their deception (See Acts 5:1-10) yet still people continued to be saved and added to the number:

> No one else dared join them, even though they were highly regarded by the people. Nevertheless, more and more men and women believed in the Lord and were added to their number.
> (Acts 5:13-14)

Returning to the Martyn Lloyd Jones quote above (which was also used at the end of the last chapter) I believe that the church will become more and more prominent and attractive as we get closer to the second coming of Jesus. As we have already briefly considered the Church being the Bride of Christ, I do not believe that the church will only be glorious once the wedding of the Bride and the Bridegroom has taken place. I have faith that Jesus, just like any bridegroom-to-be, will want to show off and display His Bride to all the world even before the wedding takes place – and to some extent this is already happening.

A Great Harvest (1) - The Prominence of the Church

The massive advancements that the church has made down through the millennia since its inception at Pentecost, coupled with the millions upon millions of people who have come to faith and trust in Jesus, have served to underpin Jesus' words to His disciples at Caesarea Philippi:

> … on this rock I will build my church, and the gates of Hades will not overcome it. (Matthew 16:18)

There will come a time when the church will be totally triumphant in its calling, with the culmination of its mission in and to the world.

As the verse above says, it will be Jesus who builds His church – using people such as you and I, (which I expand in Ch 12 – *The Church as a Building Site)* and He will not be unsuccessful in this mission given to Him by God. The triumphant work that Jesus achieved on the Cross and His subsequent resurrection served to give notice to the powers and authorities in the heavenly realms that all things were now subjected to Him.

> And He is the head of the body, the church; He is the beginning and the firstborn from among the dead, so that in everything He might have the supremacy. (Colossians 1:18)
>
> And having disarmed the powers and authorities, He made a public spectacle of them, triumphing over them by the cross. (Colossians 2:15)
>
> And God placed all things under His feet and appointed Him to be head over everything for the church. (Ephesians 1:22)

These three verses show that (1) Jesus absolutely triumphed over all that set itself up against Him and (2) everything is now subject to Him and is in submission to Him. Indeed, even before the Cross, everything was in submission to God, as we see in the book of Job when satan (I will not give him a capital letter for his name – a personal idiosyncrasy!) had to ask God for permission to test Job:

> The LORD said to satan, "Very well, then, everything he has is in your power, but on the man, himself do not lay a finger." (Job 1:12)

His Intent

> The LORD said to satan, "Very well, then, he is in your hands; but you must spare his life." (Job 2:6)

And the devil also had to ask Jesus for permission to test Peter:

> "Simon, Simon, satan has asked to sift all of you as wheat. But I have prayed for you, Simon, that your faith may not fail. And when you have turned back, strengthen your brothers." (Luke 22:31-32)

Jesus' work on the Cross, however, emphasises once and for all that all things are subject to Him – even death and Hades themselves:

> "I am the Living One; I was dead, and now look, I am alive for ever and ever! And I hold the keys of death and Hades". (Revelation 1:18)

So then, the Church has, as its Head, a victorious, conquering Lord and Saviour. I want to reiterate this as we, the Church, should be filled with boldness and encouragement, knowing Jesus is with us and He cannot be overcome or defeated.

As we saw in the previous chapter, in Paul's letter to the Ephesian Church he gives this instruction and endorsement:

> Husbands, love your wives, just as Christ loved the church and gave Himself up for her to make her holy, cleansing her by the washing with water through the word, and to present her to Himself as a radiant church, without stain or wrinkle or any other blemish, but holy and blameless. (Ephesians 5:26-27)

Strong's Exhaustive Concordance says about this work of making holy or sanctifying:

> it means to set apart, this can mean achieve dedication and service to God or the act of regarding or honouring as holy.[2]

---

2 Strong's Exhaustive Concordance – hagiazō G37

Because of His triumph on the Cross and His resurrection, Jesus will be successful in bringing to completion the work He started.

> Let us fix our eyes on Jesus, the author and perfecter of faith, who for the joy set before Him endured the cross, scorning its shame, and sat down at the right hand of the throne of God.' (Hebrews 12:2)

As Jesus hung on the Cross, He foresaw down through the ages, amongst other things, the Church, His Bride in all her glory and this vision enabled Him to endure the agonies He was going through. He will achieve this holiness and sanctifying work through the word, that is the *rhema* word – the spoken word of God.

As we have seen, Jesus encouraged His disciples by telling them the gates of Hades would not stand against the soon to emerge church. This should fill us, His people, with joy and expectation and be spurred on to accomplish all that Jesus has for His Church. The washing with water signifies a purifying, the process of making something holy.

A Time of Preparation

In the Old Testament, articles in the tabernacle and temple were sanctified and purified through sprinkling with blood, but also through washing with water before entering service for God. The priests also went through a progression of readying for service. Leviticus 8 tells us about the ordination of Aaron and his sons, which involved them first being washed with water, then being dressed in the priestly garments, after which they were sprinkled with some of the anointing oil and the blood of the ram for ordination to make them holy.

Jesus will present the church to Himself as a radiant church, without stain or wrinkle or any other blemish, but holy and blameless. (Ephesians 5:27) This again refers back to the offerings that Moses, Aaron, his sons and other priests made before God. The lamb or ram had to be perfect without defect. It is also a reference to Jesus, who John the Baptist describes as:

the Lamb of God who takes away the sin of the world.
(John 1:29)

Jesus then, in essence, will be saying to all who look at the church, "Here is the Bride My Father has given Me. Is she not beautiful?"

The church will become holy before Jesus. He will carry out a work in the church in preparation for the wedding. This preparation will take a long time. Indeed, it has been going on down through the ages since the church was birthed at Pentecost – see Acts Chapter 2.

In biblical times, this preparation period before a wedding could take as much as a year, or maybe more. The book of Esther is a story of God positioning one of His people in a place of influence to represent His people. Esther, a Jew, is chosen to be one of the prospective candidates for a Queen to King Xerxes. (The process of choosing a Queen was a lot different in those days!) As part of the process there was a time of preparation:

> Before a young woman's turn came to go in to King Xerxes, she had to complete twelve months of beauty treatments prescribed for the women, six months with oil of myrrh and six with perfumes and cosmetics. And this is how she would go to the king: Anything she wanted was given her to take with her from the harem to the king's palace. (Esther 2:12-13)

We can see, therefore, that the preparation process wasn't a hurried exercise. So also, the preparation of the church as The Bride for the Bridegroom will not be a hurried process. There will be a time when Jesus, having accomplished all that the Father set Him to do, will present the church to the Father. But until that time arrives there is still much to be accomplished through the church.

The Prominence of the Church

If we look at some synonyms for the word *prominence,* we find, amongst others, these descriptors: *outstanding, noticeable, easily seen, pronounced, in the foreground, eye catching, standing out.* In some places in the world the church today exemplifies these meanings, however in most towns and cities the church on the whole has been pushed into the background. Not, I hasten to add, that it is not doing valuable work and changing people's lives, but the majority of people have no real idea what the church is for or what it does. Their view of the church is probably shaped primarily by what they have seen on TV or in films. They may have gone to church or Sunday School when younger, however, this is becoming less and less the norm.

In the town where I live, the common issue for the church leaders, no matter what the denomination, is how to attract families and children to church activities and services.

Now some readers may say "The church is not here to be on show to people but as long as Jesus knows what we are doing then that is what matters". However, I do not think this is what Jesus wants for His Bride. Isaiah 61 speaks about God's people being oaks of righteousness:

> 'They will be called oaks of righteousness, a planting of the Lord
> for the *display* of His splendour'
> (Isaiah 61:3b my emphasis)

and we can and should apply this to the church and God's people today. We see that Isaiah calls God's people *'oaks of righteousness'*. Oak trees conjure up an image of strength and solidity. a tree that is not easily uprooted. One of the qualities of oak as a building material is its durability. Many towns and cities still have some oak framed buildings which have been around since the 1500's. Whilst the Hebrew word for oak (*ayil*) can mean any large tree, the use of the word 'oak' in the NIV is especially helpful. Oak trees grow in around 500 species and are found across a wide area of the world, including the Americas, Europe, Asia and North Africa.

I find it fascinating that the compilers of the NIV and other versions should use the word '*oak*' in this verse. It speaks of God's people across the world being like oak trees - dependable, solid in their faith, with great spiritual strength.

The website *BIOS* – a manufacturer of biodegradable products says of the oak tree,

> 'It's a symbol of strength, morale, resistance and knowledge. Throughout history, the Oak has been represented in different mythologies and sometimes linked to powerful gods (in Greek mythology it was a symbol of Zeus, the God of Thunder.) The oak is considered a **cosmic storehouse** of wisdom embodied in its towering strength. It grows slowly, but surely at its own rate. Oak is often associated with honour, nobility, and wisdom as well thanks to its size and longevity. Oaks are known to easily surpass 300 years of age making it a powerful life-affirming symbol. The oak is a living legend representing all that is true, wholesome, stable, and noble.'[3]

So, I do not see this as being a mistake that the compilers of the NIV have chosen to use the phrase *oaks of righteousness'* to describe God's people.

Isaiah 61:3 also says that God's people are *'for the display of His splendour'* and again this is, I believe, quite significant. It speaks of God's people, the Church, showing God's splendour, majesty and beauty to those around them. I do not see this as only being once we are in glory. I sense this happening at some point in the church's future ministry here on earth. Yes, this is happening in some places around the world but I am seeing that this will become far more widespread and visible in a time to come.

As I have already stated, I firmly believe, that God's Church is yet to achieve its fullness and prominence in the society in which we live and serve God. Jesus still has much to accomplish through His church, and it would seem that the best years are yet to come. It may appear unimaginable after all that has been already been achieved in the 2000 years since the church's inception, with the millions of people who have come into a saving knowledge of Jesus, many of whom have been martyred for their faith, but there is yet still more to come and to be achieved by God's people.

---

[3] Bios Urn Environment SL

Chapter Three

A Great Harvest (2) - A Place for Revival

The desert and the parched land will be glad; the wilderness will rejoice and blossom. (Isaiah 35:1)

Desert, parched land, wilderness. Each of these adjectives portray a place that is lacking in rain and has no obvious signs of fertility: the soil or dust just is not fit for anything to grow in. Whether they have always been in that condition or they have become like that because of changes to the climate or mis- use by mankind we do not know. They are dry, arid places. Few people, if any, live there. We can't be sure whether Isaiah was seeing these places in his mind's eye, or if he was hearing the words whispered to his heart by the Holy Spirit. But they vividly convey the scene.

Whilst these descriptions refer to a physical land, having preached on this chapter in the past, whilst preparing for the message I saw that the above description can also refer to the spiritual landscape of a town or city. Many readers may well be able to identify with this situation.

Interestingly, some of the verses in Psalm 107 might shed some light on why there is this barrenness:

> "He turned rivers into a desert, flowing springs into thirsty ground, and fruitful land into a salt waste, because of the wickedness of those who lived there." (Psalm 107:33-34)

As I have just mentioned, when I was preparing for preaching on this chapter, God showed me that the verses in Isaiah 35:1-2 could apply to the spiritual state of our villages, towns and cities. If this is the situation, bearing in mind the information in Psalm 107:33-34, then could it not also be the case that God has deliberately caused the spiritual condition of our nation to be as it is, by withdrawing His presence and favour because of the wickedness of its people? Or at least, perhaps, He has allowed this scenario to come about for some other reason.

A Great Harvest (2) – The Place for Revival

In Romans Chapter 1, three times we read the phrase *God gave them over*, (vs 24, 26, 28) in referring to people's sinful desires, lusts and depraved minds. It would seem therefore, that God at times, stands back and allows people to 'get on with it'. As the saying goes, 'they've made their beds to lie on'.

Now granted there are many, many God-fearing followers of Jesus in the town's cities and villages throughout the UK, and within these places there are many flourishing churches. However, as a whole, the people of God in this country are still in the minority with witnessing and seeing people come to faith seeming to be an uphill struggle.

Now you may point out that we have not been promised an easy ride in our evangelistic efforts, but there does seem to be a great resistance - something of a barrier, even, to getting people to show a modicum of interest in the Christian faith. Yet in the verses in Isaiah 61 we see that this situation is not without hope. There is a promise that these conditions will not always remain so:

> "Like the crocus it (the wilderness) will burst into bloom; it will rejoice greatly and shout for joy. The glory of Lebanon will be given to it, the splendour of Carmel and Sharon; they will see the glory of the LORD, the splendour of our God."
> (Isaiah 35:2 - my emphasis)

Carmel, Sharon and Lebanon were rich, fertile regions with thickly wooded areas. People would readily identify with Isaiah's picture as the areas he was referring to were well known in the region. God was saying through the prophet, that though the areas looked bleak, He was going to bring about remarkable change.

An End-Time Harvest?

Towards the end of his life, Smith Wigglesworth, the 19th/20th century evangelist and healer, prophesied about an end-time harvest, part of which said:

> "When the new church phase is on the wane, there will be evidence in the churches of something that has not been seen

> before: a coming together of those with an emphasis on the word and those with an emphasis on the Spirit. When the word and the Spirit come together, there will be the biggest move of the Holy Spirit that the nation, and indeed, the world has ever seen. It will mark the beginning of a revival that will eclipse anything that has been witnessed within these shores, even the Wesleyan and Welsh revivals of former years. The outpouring of God's Spirit will flow over from the United Kingdom to mainland Europe, and from there, will begin a missionary move to the ends of the earth."[4]

Will there be an end-time harvest or revival? There surely is a great need for God to sweep through our towns and cities with His revival fire given the spiritual state of them. Is it possible that the Lord of all the earth, will usher in a mighty harvest of souls that will out-strip all that has so far been achieved?

Admittedly, Wigglesworth's prophecy doesn't explicitly say it will be *the* end-time harvest or revival but it does indicate something quite significant for God's Church.

The Old Testament book of Hosea encourages God's people to return to Him, even though they have experienced His discipline, with the promise that He will restore, refresh and revive them like winter and spring rains. (Some early versions have latter and former rains):

> "Come, let us return to the Lord. He has torn us to pieces but He will heal us; He has injured us but He will bind up our wounds. After two days He will revive us; on the third day He will restore us, that we may live in His presence. Let us acknowledge the Lord; let us press on to acknowledge Him. As surely as the sun rises, He will appear; He will come to us like the winter rains, like the spring rains that water the earth."
> (Hosea 6:1-3)

I believe that past revivals give us a snapshot of God's great love for humankind. Central to revivals has been the work of the Holy Spirit.

---

[4] Smith Wigglesworth prophecy–Revival Fires and Awakenings by Mathew Backholer, ByFaith Media, 2009, 2017, pages 189-190.

A Great Harvest (2) – The Place for Revival

We read in Acts 2 of how the Holy Spirit came to rest upon the 120 believers gathered in a house and that they were changed from cowering, frightened disciples into bold witnesses for Jesus.

Later, in subsequent chapters of the book of Acts we see the Holy Spirit enabling the disciples to boldly carry out the works as Jesus did – indeed as He said they would do (John 14:12). This work then becomes more prominent during times of revival. I am not saying that some of this work isn't being done in the church during periods outside of revival times. Indeed, the vast majority of God's work carries on quietly in the everyday life of the church. In addition, many towns, cities and countries have never experienced revival of any sort, yet the church continues to thrive and to flourish.

Where there has been a revival of some kind, the church takes on a marked significance within the community it serves. Reports during the 1904–05 Welsh revival said that magistrates and police had 'quieter times' as the drunkards had been converted and crime as a whole was markedly reduced or non-existent! It is this marked significance that I bring to the reader's attention when speaking about the prominence of the church in the last days before Jesus returns.

There has been a cry from the church worldwide over the centuries, for God to come and sweep the nations. In His mercy, He has sent His Holy Spirit in waves down through the history of the church, and large numbers of people have become Christians. Perhaps the most well-known revival in the British Isles was that in Wales, 1904-1905 where it is estimated 100,000 people gave their lives to Christ in packed meetings.

Late in the 20th century at Brownsville Assemblies of God church, in Pensacola, Florida, God began a work on Father's Day, 18th June 1995. Over the course of two years over 200,000 people become Christians and many more recommitted their lives to Jesus.

Why God sends the Holy Spirit to certain churches, areas or whole countries (as seen with Wales on several occasions) is not totally known or understood. Some of these visitations can be traced to a prolonged season of prayer for a particular area e.g., Brownsville Assembly of God church, Pensacola started with a Sunday evening prayer meeting for revival, which ran for some three years before it happened.

In the Scottish Outer Hebrides, two faithful sisters, Peggy and Christine Smith, prayed for months in 1949 for the village of Barvas. In addition, unaware of this, seven men were also meeting three nights a week to pray for their village and surrounding area. As a result of these faithful, praying Christians, God visited the islands over the course of the next three years, bringing thousands to faith in Jesus. While the island population was small, the effect of the revival as it spread across the region and beyond was experienced by many thousands of people.

There have been many, many books written on the subject of revival and I have several on my bookshelves. They contain documented accounts of numerous revivals that have taken place down through the ages.

If you have ever been at a railway station, airport or dockside there always seem to be those who are in a rush to get their means of transport. At a rail terminus, an announcement comes over the tannoy, "the train now leaving platform 3 is the train for Manchester Piccadilly" Sure enough, there will be those, hurrying down the platform to try and catch their train as it starts to edge out of the station.

I enjoy watching documentaries on TV about airports. Having flown to several parts of the world I have developed a love of travel, so when there is a programme about an airport such as Heathrow in London, I like to tune in. Invariably there is a part of the programme where several announcements are given calling certain passengers to their departure gate which is about to close.

In thinking about the end of the age, and whether there will be an end-time harvest, it would seem to me that God in His great mercy and love will bring about a massive increase in the work of evangelism. Great numbers of people will be ushered into the kingdom of God – a bit like those last few passengers hurrying for their train or plane.

A Great Harvest (2) – The Place for Revival

God is a merciful God and longs that none should perish. In his first letter to his disciple Timothy, Paul gives him instruction about praying for everyone, that we may live peaceful lives. In particular, he writes:

> "This is good (prayers, intercession and thanksgiving be made for everyone) and pleases God our Saviour, who wants all people to be saved and to come to a knowledge of the truth."
> (1 Timothy 2:3-4 - my insertion)

Note that Paul writes that God wants *all people to be saved.* This is the mercy of God.

The apostle Peter in his second letter to the people of God also takes up this truth:

> "The Lord is not slow in keeping His promise, as some understand slowness. Instead, He is patient with you, **not wanting anyone to perish,** but everyone to come to repentance." (2 Peter 3:9 – my emphasis)

Now I am not saying that the two verses above mean that all *will* be saved. However, it does show God's heart for people and His desire that they be saved. But the onus will still be very much on individuals to accept this message of salvation. God will not bend the rules or make exceptions for these last few people to be saved.

Should it not surprise us that God in His great mercy would give a final call for people to be saved? Is it not within His great grace to send the Holy Spirit to bring about that saving work and raise faith in people's hearts to accept Jesus as Lord and Saviour?

> "For it is by grace you have been saved, through faith - and this is not from yourselves, it is the gift of God."
> (Ephesians 2:18)

It is through God's grace that we are saved, and as Paul says in the verse above, this grace is a gift from God. What better demonstration of His immeasurable grace than bringing people into a saving knowledge of His Son, Jesus?

In Acts 4 we read about Peter and John being brought before the Sanhedrin. They had healed a man at the gate Beautiful at the Temple, and had been preaching about Jesus. As they are questioned about how they had healed the man, Peter, filled with the Holy Spirit says:

> "Salvation is found in no-one else, for there is no other name under heaven given to people by which we must be saved." (Acts 4:12)

There is absolutely no other name or way by which we can be saved, other than in and through the Name of Jesus. Many people try other ways, but they fall short of what is required, namely:

> "If you declare with your mouth, 'Jesus is Lord,' and believe in your heart that God raised Him from the dead, you will be saved. For it is with your heart that you believe and are justified, and it is with your mouth that you profess your faith and are saved." (Romans 10:9-10)

So, it is my belief and understanding that there will be many, many people finally saved at the end of time and this will still be through faith and trust in God's Son, Jesus.

Preparation

At harvest times in the fields surrounding the town where I live in the South West of England, there is much activity taking place. The crops are ready to be harvested and the farmers make sure they use every hour in the day. During this harvest period it is not unusual, if driving along a road late in an evening, to find a tractor with a trailer full of harvested grain or bales of straw heading to the stores and barns.

I know from speaking in the past with farmers, that they take on extra workers to help get the harvest in before the autumn rains come. They work long hours, but the farming communities recognise that with only a short period of about six weeks, the harvest has to be gathered if it is not to be ruined by the September rains.

A Great Harvest (2) – The Place for Revival

Jesus recognised the importance of the need for workers for the harvest. He taught His disciples:

> "The harvest is plentiful but the workers are few. Ask the Lord of the harvest, therefore, to send out workers into His harvest field." (Matthew 9:37-38)

Here, He is saying that this is an important time and that extra workers are needed. To harvest means to reap or gather in. It is widely believed that in the verse above, Jesus is referring to Himself, although there are some who think this refers to God the Father. Irrespective of who it might be, Jesus bids us to pray and ask for more workers to be sent out into the harvest field.

One morning after I had drafted this chapter, I was praying and asking the Lord about what I had written. As I prayed, I found myself saying the words, *"compel them to come in."* I knew immediately where this phrase came from. It is found in Luke 14:15-24, the parable of the Great Banquet. Jesus is at the home of a prominent Pharisee and has been giving them teaching on where to sit if they are invited to a wedding feast. (It would seem in those days they didn't have place settings with name cards as most weddings do nowadays.)

After this teaching, someone says in v15, *"Blessed is the one who will eat at the feast in the kingdom of God"* (referring to the resurrection of the righteous that Jesus has just spoken of). In reply, Jesus tells another parable. He speaks about a great banquet being held and the guests who are invited. However, one by one, they begin to make excuses as to why they cannot come. One has just got married, another has bought a field and has to go and see it. Still another has bought some oxen and needs to try them out. The owner of the house gets angry and says to his servants,

> "Go out quickly into the streets and alleys of the town and bring in the poor, the crippled, the blind and the lame."
> (Luke 14:21)

This done, the servants tell him:

"What you have ordered has been done, but there is still room." (v22)

Here's where the Holy Spirit spoke to me:

> "Then the master told his servant, 'Go out to the roads and country lanes and **make them come in**, so that my house will be full" (v23 – my emphasis)

The phrase "make them come in" (or *compel them to come in* in some versions) speaks of an urgency and determination for this to be done. The Greek word for *compel* that is used here is *anankazo*.[5] This has the inference to drive, to constrain, to entreat or to impel by force.

With the use of this word we can see, that Jesus was placing great emphasis and significance on what He was saying about this last in-gathering of souls. It is my belief that this is what the parable is all about.

As we come to the end of this chapter, I just want to draw your attention to some verses in the book of Revelation:

> "Then another angel came out of the temple and called in a loud voice to him who was sitting on the cloud, 'Take your sickle and reap, because the time to reap has come, for the harvest of the earth is ripe.' So, he who was seated on the cloud swung his sickle over the earth, and the earth was harvested."
> (Revelation 14:15-16)

Now, there are different schools of thought on these and the next two verses. Various commentaries have diverse interpretations of them. However, as I have read, studied and prayed over this meaning, I believe that the verses above refer to a harvesting of souls, with this first angel being commanded to reap for the harvest is ripe. (Possibly cross referencing to Matthew 9:37).

We then read:

---

5 anankazō – Strong's Exhaustive Concordance G315

> "Another angel came out of the temple in heaven, and he too had a sharp sickle. Still another angel, who had charge of the fire, came from the altar and called in a loud voice to him who had the sharp sickle, 'Take your sharp sickle and gather the clusters of grapes from the earth's vine, because its grapes are ripe.' The angel swung his sickle on the earth, gathered its grapes and threw them into the great winepress of God's wrath." (Revelation 14:17-19)

The second angel is commanded to gather the grapes of God's wrath (judgement). While in the gospels, Jesus does speak of God's judgement, He also spoke much about God's mercy and heart for the lost and His desire to bring in those who will be saved. There is no hint of the wrath of God with the first harvest.

The parable of weeds in Matthew Chapter 13 has similarities to our verses from Revelation 14. In the parable a field is sown and the crop grows up, but weeds also grow among the wheat. Asked by the servants if they should pull up the weeds, the farmer says:

> "No, because while you are pulling up the weeds you may uproot the wheat". (Matthew 13:29)

Later, the disciples ask Jesus to explain the parable, where He says:

> "The Son of Man will send out His angels, and they will weed out of His kingdom everything that causes sin and all who do evil. They will throw them into the blazing furnace, where there will be weeping and gnashing of teeth. Then the righteous will shine like the sun in the kingdom of their Father. Whoever has ears, let them hear." (Matthew 13:41-43)

In the passage in Revelation 14 we see that it is Jesus – 'the son of man' – the Lord of the harvest, who reaps this harvest.

Many see these two events as being one and the same: namely the harvest of judgement, but for the reasons given above, I disagree with this interpretation. Although it is not in the text, the word *'then'* could be placed at the beginning of v17 as I see the work of gathering being separate to the harvest carried out by the angels in vs 14-16. I therefore see this as an indicator that there will be some form of large-scale work of God to bring people into His kingdom before the final judgement.

In Part II, when we study Ephesians 3:10, let us keep in mind also the verses from Hosea that there is still yet a glorious future for the church here on earth:

> "Come, let us return to the Lord. He has torn us to pieces but He will heal us; He has injured us but He will bind up our wounds. After two days He will revive us; on the third day He will restore us, that we may live in His presence. Let us acknowledge the Lord; let us press on to acknowledge Him. As surely as the sun rises, He will appear; He will come to us like the winter rains, like the spring rains that water the earth." (Hosea 6:1-3)

Chapter Four

A Wedding Planned

Throughout its entirety the Bible is, about the planning of a wedding. This is no ordinary wedding though. It is about the wedding of Christ and His glorious church. Although the Old Testament doesn't make this at first clear, it is about God's intent for His Son, Jesus. He will take for Himself a bride, in whom He would be honoured and delighted with, and whom He would show off to all the world and the heavenly realms.

Right at the outset, when we read in Genesis Chapter 2 of the first marriage - that of Adam and Eve, this is in actuality an illustration of the marriage of Christ and His church. We shall consider this in the later chapters of this book.

The whole Bible is an account of God's great love for people and how He has called many, many millions down through the ages to be a part of His plan to have a people called His own.

As we read through the Bible, we see in the first instance the gathering and wooing of the people of Israel to be called His own, but they reject Him and His love, preferring to go their own way.

However, God would not and did not disown them. He continued to care for them, telling them repeatedly how much He loved them and wanted them, by sending His messengers, the prophets. Yet still the people of Israel, by and large, would not listen. At times they turned back to God, but, sadly, it didn't last and they again wandered off to worship other gods and idols.

God's master plan all along was for His Son Jesus to be revealed to the world and to bring an even greater number of people to Himself. These people would be known as the Church and would not only encompass the Jews who put their faith in Jesus, but also the Gentiles - those not of the Jewish (or Israelite) heritage, who came to believe in Jesus. This church would be the bride of God's Son, Jesus.

Christ is woven throughout the Old Testament. Several passages in the New Testament refer back to this aspect. For example,

> "Through Him (that is Jesus - my addition) all things were made; without Him nothing was made that has been made." (John 1:3)

> "For by Him things in heaven and on earth, visible and invisible, whether thrones or powers or rulers or authorities; all things have been created by Him and for Him." (Colossians 1:16)

> "but in these last days He has spoken to us by his Son, whom He appointed heir of all things, and through whom also He made the universe." (Hebrews 1:2)

We see in these three scriptures that although God created the earth, the Holy Spirit reveals to the New Testament writers that it was Jesus who carried out this work, under God the Father's direction.

Elsewhere in the New Testament we see other references to Jesus' work in Old Testament times:

> "Though you already know all this, I want to remind you that the Lord at one time delivered His people out of Egypt, but later destroyed those who did not believe." (Jude v5)

and there is a footnote in the NIV that says 'some early manuscripts *Jesus*' (substituted for 'Lord')

Isaiah saw Jesus' glory when he had his vision of the throne of God. (Isaiah 6) In his Gospel, John refers to Isaiah 6:10 in Chapter 12:41 when he notes:

> "Isaiah said this because he saw Jesus' glory and spoke about Him." (John 12:41)

Jesus isn't just *promised* in the Old Testament, He is actually *present* in the Old Testament!

The Betrothal

As we saw in Chapter One with our opening illustration of a typical English wedding (recognising that similar ceremonies happen in many other parts of the world) there is a time of courtship. The future bride and groom recognising a mutual attraction begin a period of getting to know each other, eventually leading to love, affection and commitment to a future marriage.

The word 'betrothal' is not in common English usage nowadays. We instead use the term 'engaged' to indicate the intention between two people to become married. In Old Testament times the courtship period was totally different to what we know – certainly here in the West today.

In those days, a couple would have been brought together by their respective fathers or other influential male relatives (very much a male dominated lifestyle.)

In the Bible we see some examples of this style of arrangement. In Genesis 24 we read the story of how Isaac and Rebekah came to be husband and wife. Reading through this account, neither Isaac or Rebekah had any real involvement in the process until they were 'introduced' by the (nameless) chief servant of Abraham. It seems very strange to us nowadays that the intended couple had no real say in the matter of who they might wed, but it appears to have worked, for they were soon married.

Although they struggled to have children for the first twenty years of their marriage, they eventually conceived and had two sons, Jacob (who was later renamed Israel by God), and Esau. In the account of Isaac and Rebekah it is interesting the importance of prayer and dependence on God, to guide the servant in finding the right bride for his master.

When we read some of the parables of Jesus, we can now perhaps begin to understand the customs of the day. When Jesus told His disciples the parable of the ten virgins (Matthew 25:1-13), He used an everyday example that they would have easily understood.

A Wedding Planned

In the Gospels of Matthew (1:18) and Luke (1:27 & 2:5) we read that Mary was pledged or betrothed to Joseph. When Mary became pregnant through the Holy Spirit, Joseph had it in mind to divorce her quietly so as not to disgrace her. This showed the nature and uprightness of Joseph – Matthew 1:19 says that he was a righteous man, as he had every right to make a great issue of this pregnancy which he had no part in.

The betrothal looked to be in serious trouble, with Joseph believing that Mary had slept with another man and wanting to 'put her away'. It took the intervention of God through a dream and an angel to convince Joseph that this wasn't the case and that this pregnancy was God's work.

So, we see that the betrothal of a man and woman was a solemn undertaking and not entered into lightly. Why have I taken time to explain this betrothal process? What does it have to do with Jesus and His church? Well, in actual fact, this analogy of God's people being the Bride of His Son, Jesus, carries through the Old Testament, Hosea Chapter Two (NIV) has the heading, *Israel Punished and Restored.* The nation of Israel were the chosen people of God who rebelled and disobeyed God.

Through the prophet Hosea, God tells His people that they will be punished for their disobedience, but will later be restored. As part of this restoration promise God says:

> "Therefore, I am now going to allure her; I will lead her into the wilderness and speak tenderly to her. There I will give her back her vineyards, and will make the Valley of Achor a door of hope. There she will respond as in the days of her youth, as in the day she came up out of Egypt. In that day,' declares the Lord, 'you will call me 'my husband'; you will no longer call me 'my master." (Hosea 2:14-16)

"In that day," declares the LORD, "you will call me 'my husband'; you will no longer call me 'my master," (vs 16), shows God's loving intentions towards His people. Today, the whole church is called His people. Now, all of God's people can call Him *"her husband."*

A Promised Bride

In John's Gospel - Chapter 3:27-30 we read that John the Baptist introduces the concept of Jesus being the bridegroom within the background of the marriage process of their day:

> "The bride belongs to the bridegroom. The friend who attends the bridegroom waits and listens for him, and is full of joy when he hears the bridegroom's voice. That joy is mine, and it is now complete." (John 3:29)

John the Baptist is saying here that he is the friend, Jesus is the Bridegroom and John's joy is now complete that the promised Messiah is now here.

So, if Jesus is the Bridegroom who then, is the Bride? In Paul's second letter to the Corinthian church, he writes:

> "I am jealous for you with a godly jealousy. I promised you to one husband, to Christ, so that I might present you as a pure virgin to Him." (2 Corinthians 11:2)

Now, although Paul is writing to the church in Corinth, it is not just the Corinthian church he is speaking of as being promised to Jesus, but he has the God given authority to speak for the whole church in general as being promised to Jesus as His bride.

The word 'promised' is *harmozō*[6] in the Greek and has the same meaning as 'pledged' or 'espoused' which we saw with Mary being pledged or betrothed to Joseph.

So, Paul is saying here that the church as a whole is pledged, promised or betrothed to Jesus as His bride.

In his letter to the Ephesian church Paul writes in Chapter 5 about husbands and wives:

---

6 harmozō Strong's Exhaustive Concordance – G718

> "Husbands, love your wives, just as Christ loved the church and gave Himself up for her to make her holy, cleansing her by the washing with water through the word, and to present her to Himself as a radiant church, without stain or wrinkle or any other blemish, but holy and blameless. In this same way, husband's ought to love their wives as their own bodies. He who loves his wife loves himself. After all, no one ever hated their own body, but they feed and care for their body, just as Christ does the church - for we are members of His body. 'For this reason, a man will leave his father and mother and be united to his wife, and the two will become one flesh.'" This is a profound mystery - but I am talking about Christ and the church." (Ephesians 5:25-32)

Now, these verses have caused great controversy down through the centuries in how husbands and wives should behave toward each other, but the point I want to make here is that these verses are, in reality, about Christ as the Bridegroom and the church as His Bride. Paul makes this clear in v32 where he acknowledges that this is a profound mystery but clarifies and emphasises the point he is making – that he is talking about Christ and the church.

So, we can see that there is a loving relationship between Jesus and His church and that the church is the promised bride for Jesus.

Note also in v25 above that Paul says Jesus loves the church and makes her holy and radiant. This is the future in store for the church – the glorious future. The church will not, as some think, crawl across the finishing line, dispirited, bedraggled, thoroughly beaten and cowed at the final coming together with Jesus as His bride, but she will be glorious and radiant (v27).

If we were a guest at the wedding described in chapter 1 – *The Bride,* and on her entry the bride showed up in a wedding dress that was torn, covered in dirt and mud, with her bridal veil askew, hair dishevelled, a broken heel on one shoe, what would be the rection of the congregation? There would be a collective gasp of horror. People would perhaps faint in shock. Others would look away ashamed. All in all, not what was expected at all. Perhaps this might be portrayed in a comedy TV programme or film but not at all in real life (although there may have been the odd real-life occasion where this has happened).

This is a picture of the church that God gave me many years ago. It was so vivid that I can still see it now as if it had just been given to me. I knew when I saw the picture it related to Jesus and His bride, the church. I discerned also that this wasn't what was going to happen with the church at the end of time. I knew that as a bride on her wedding day is dressed to bring out her beauty and inner loveliness, so it will be with the church. Ephesians 5:27 as we have seen above, says that the church will be presented to Jesus as a radiant bride.

Jesus triumphed on the Cross for the church, His Bride. He fought tooth and nail for the church. He smashed the opposition that satan threw at Him completely. I particularly love the verses in Colossians:

> "Christ forgave us all our sins, having cancelled the written code, with its regulations that was against us and stood opposed to us; He has taken it away, nailing it to the cross. And having disarmed the powers and authorities, **He made a public spectacle of them,** triumphing over them by the cross." (Colossians 2:13b - 15 - my emphasis)

Jesus completely and utterly defeated the devil and all his hordes of demons. They knew it then and still know it today. It is for the church to wake up and recognise that we have a glorious future ahead of us. Many have tried over the centuries to close down and dismantle the church but she still keeps going, still keeps popping up much, no doubt, to satan's annoyance.

Revelation 19 gives us an insight into the life after Jesus returns to claim His bride:

> "Let us rejoice and be glad and give Him glory! For the wedding of the Lamb has come, and His bride has made herself ready. Fine linen, bright and clean, was given her to wear. (Fine linen stands for the righteous acts of God's holy people.)" (Revelation 19:7-8)

Here, we see that Jesus, as the Lamb of God, has come for His bride. This then is the glorious future the church can look forward to. We will expand this aspect of the church in the next chapter.

Chapter Five

What is the Church?

In the previous chapters we have seen what I believe is God's end-time plan for His church. It would therefore, be appropriate at this juncture to look at what we mean by church, what it is and what its function is.

There are thousands of different churches spread across the world. From the established Anglican and Roman Catholic churches that have existed for hundreds of years, through to the pillars of the Methodist and Baptist church. Then there are the Pentecostal, the charismatic churches and the independent churches found in hundreds of towns, cities and villages. Not forgetting also tiny clusters of believers scattered in remote areas in places virtually unknown to anyone except God the Father Himself.

Each church has a certain flavour, which may stem from established traditions and practices, but also many will simply be trying to follow the guidance found in the Bible. Countless churches comprise only a few dedicated followers of Jesus, faithfully meeting together in many different places. These meeting places range from purpose-built church buildings, to schools, theatres, cinemas and a variety of other venues. Then there is the house church movement, seeking to follow the early church model which we read of in Acts Chapter 2 and several other places in the Scriptures.

There are those Christians who have to meet secretly in underground places or in the open air in forests or woodlands so as to avoid prying eyes ready to inform authorities. All these go to make up the tapestry of God's people, for, as we shall see, the church is made up of people, rather than buildings as many associate the church with.

But what does the Bible say about God's Church? Jesus told His disciples:

What is the Church?

"**I** will build **My** church and the gates of hell will not prevail against it" (Matthew 16:18 my emphasis)

So, where do we start in our exploration of what the church is and does?

As we have just seen, it was Jesus who introduced this new body of people known as the church. The New Testament was written in Greek and the word for church is *ekklēsia,* which means a congregation, an assembly or group of people gathered together. This word was already in use in Jesus' time. He didn't come up with something that would take time to explain to His disciples but He used a word that they would easily understand. Indeed, after Jesus made His statement about building His church, there isn't anything recorded where the disciples asked Him what He meant. They completely 'got it'!

It is worth observing that the entry in Strong's Exhaustive Concordance for *ekklēsia*[7] clarifies that in the New Testament a church is never a building or meeting place. The word *ekklēsia* can refer to a totality, where Paul points out it is through the church the manifold wisdom of God is made known (Ephesians 3:10) or to a specific location:

> "Give my greetings to the brethren at Laodicea, and to Nympha **and the church in her house**" (Colossians 4:15 – my emphasis).

So, when Jesus told His disciples that He would build His church He wasn't referring to a building but to a body of people.

The word or term *ekklēsia* also means 'called out', and in those days was commonly used to indicate an assembly of Greek citizens. The early church would have been well aware of the significance of being 'called out' by God into their new found faith. In addition, the Hebrew word *qahel*[8], found in the Old Testament seventeen times, also means 'an assembly'. Since Jesus would have spoken Aramaic or Hebrew it is quite likely that He used one of these words and that the Greek writers then used *ekklēsia* in their translations.

---

7 Strong's Exhaustive Concordance – ekklēsia G1577
8 Strong's Exhaustive Concordance – qahel H6951

It is worth reiterating that it is Jesus who will do the building. This might at first seem strange as He had already told them He wasn't going to be physically with them for much longer. One would have thought He would have left it to the disciples, perhaps saying to them, "You will build My church", but this is not the case. This therefore, indicated to them that He was going to be with them by His Spirit.

It is interesting to note also that there are only two references to 'church' in the Gospels; here in Matthew 16 and again in Matthew 18, when Jesus is giving teaching on discipline in the church.

It was when Luke's account in the book of Acts and letters of Paul etc were written that the word 'church' became more common when referring to the body of believers.

The Work of the Holy Spirit in the Church

Having given His disciples a 'heads up' about what is in store for them, Jesus then goes on to tell them about the work of the Holy Spirit and the mission that lies ahead. Although the various events in the gospels aren't necessarily in chronological order, we get a rounded picture when they are read in conjunction with one another. At one point, Jesus explains to His disciples about the Holy Spirit and how vital He will be to the work of the new church:

> "I will ask the Father, and He will give you another advocate to help you and be with you forever - the Spirit of truth"
> (John 14:16-17a)

The word 'advocate' used here (Greek *paraklētos*) means 'summoned' and 'called to one's side'. or called to one's aid. We can see that Jesus was telling them just how much they would need the Holy Spirit's help in the mission that He had for them. It is sufficient to say at this time, that Jesus was already planning ahead and informing the disciples about this.

The Wind of God

In Acts 2 we see the Holy Spirit giving birth to the new church that Jesus had earlier spoken about with His disciples. Although He had told them they would be His witnesses and that they were to remain in Jerusalem for the promised Holy Spirit, I guess that none of them could have imagined what this would look like. When the Holy Spirit came on them, it must have taken them completely by surprise.

In Acts 2:2 the word '*suddenly*' means as we generally understand it: namely that they were taken completely unaware. Similar to a surprise! One dictionary says that suddenly means *quickly and unexpectedly* and I'm sure that the disciples would certainly concur! Jesus didn't say how many days the disciples would have to wait in Jerusalem for the Holy Spirit. He did not give them a day or time. They had to stay there by faith and wait. There were some things to do while they waited, for example, there was a replacement to be found for the traitor and betrayer Judas (Acts 1:12-26). We can also presume that they met together over the ensuing days to try and come to terms with Jesus' ascension and what He had told them to expect.

On the day of Pentecost there were about 120 people gathered together in a house. Pentecost, meaning the fiftieth day, was already an established part of the Jewish calendar, celebrated on the fiftieth day after Passover. As the second of three great annual feasts, it celebrated and gave thanks to God for the harvest – see Leviticus 23:15-21.
Following the events of Pentecost, the church really got up and running. The first day 3000 people were saved and baptised, and people were added to their number daily (Acts 2:47). In Acts 4:4 the number rose to about 5000 men. (Sadly, although Paul greatly praised many women, recorded events in those days centred around the men). We can presume then, that with the inclusion of women and older children who came to faith, the church numbered in the region of ten thousand plus. One wonders how the apostles coped with the logistics of this early church growth!

Having held various positions of leadership in several churches, I can well appreciate the challenges the apostles faced in the rapidly expanding church. The explosion of growth in this fledgling assembly, coupled with the new teaching and freedom that the recent converts found in their new faith must have led to some sleepless nights for Peter and the apostles. Indeed, in Acts 6 we see how they dealt with one issue that raised its head: that of how to fairly distribute the daily food allocations to the widows among them. A logical, but no doubt, Holy Spirit led solution was agreed on and the first deacons were put in place to oversee the practical matters. It is noteworthy that Luke records at the end of this event:

> 'The number of disciples in Jerusalem increased **rapidly**'
> (Acts 6:7- my emphasis)

We can see that, at first, the unseasoned church grew quickly, and scriptural references give us an insight into this:

> "Nevertheless, more and more men and women believed in the Lord and were added to their number." (Acts 5:14)

> "Then the church throughout Judea, Galilee and Samaria enjoyed a time of peace and was strengthened. Living in the fear of the Lord and encouraged by the Holy Spirit, it increased in numbers."
> (Acts 9:31)

> "This became known all over Joppa, (The raising of Tabitha from the dead by Peter) and many people believed in the Lord." (Acts 9:42 - my insertion)

After reading these stirring accounts of rapid growth, we might ask ourselves the thorny question, "Why don't we still see the church growing like that in the book of Acts?" Although we may not hear about what is happening in the world, the church is still growing, and in places, at phenomenal speed.

In an article in Christianity Today in 2015, it is reported that:

> The Church has seen dramatic and explosive growth in Asia, Africa and South America. The growth of the African Church in particular is jaw-

What is the Church?

dropping. In 1900 there were fewer than 9 million Christians in Africa. Now there are more than 541 million. In the last 15 years alone, the Church in Africa has seen a 51 per cent increase, which works out on average at around 33,000 people either becoming Christians or being born into Christian families each day, in Africa alone.[9]

The World Christian Encyclopaedia estimates that 2.9 million people become Christians every year. That equates to nearly 80,000 people per day giving their lives to Jesus. He is still building His church.

The Holy Spirit is key to this work, notwithstanding that it is all carried out in the Name of Jesus. The Holy Spirit is described as being the comforter, helper, counsellor or advocate. He has been sent to teach us all things (about God the Father and Jesus the Son). He teaches us about the deep truths of the Bible and gives us understanding in so many areas of the Christian life.

The Holy Spirit produces fruit within us as we grow in our Christian lives:

> But the fruit of the Spirit is love, joy, peace, forbearance, kindness, goodness, faithfulness, gentleness and self-control. Against such things there is no law. (Galatians 5:22-23)

The Holy Spirit also gives us spiritual gifts which help us to be effective in our walk with Jesus. There are two main passages of scripture laying out a range of spiritual gifts –

> We have different gifts, according to the grace given to each of us. If your gift is prophesying, then prophesy in accordance with your faith; if it is serving, then serve; if it is teaching, then teach; if it is to encourage, then give encouragement; if it is giving, then give generously; if it is to lead, do it diligently; if it is to show mercy, do it cheerfully. (Romans 12:6-8)

In 1 Corinthians 12:1-11 Paul lists other spiritual gifts – wisdom, knowledge, faith, healing, miraculous powers, prophecy, distinguishing between spirits, speaking in tongues and interpretation of tongues.

---

9 Christianity Today magazine – March 2015

There is an additional list (sometimes referred to as ministries or offices but v 7 speaks of God giving gifts) in Ephesians 4:11 – apostles, prophets, evangelists, pastors and teachers.

There are many interpretations as to what constitutes a gift, subsequently you will find a variety of tables and lists of what might be understood as gifts of the Holy Spirit in the Bible. Depending on which list you view there can be anywhere from 7 – 25 different enablement's.

What is to be noted is that apart from prophecy (and prophet in the Ephesian 4 verses) there is no single definitive list in any of the above passages. It would seem to me therefore; these are a selection of the type of gifts the Holy Spirit distributes to people and the variety of giftings we can expect to find within the church.

There are many other gifts the Holy Spirit gives to the church that we don't find in the Bible passages, for instance the gift of intercession or worship leading.

The Church in …

It is worth noting that many of the New Testament letters were written to the whole church in a particular town or city.

The believers in those places met in various locations, including people's homes. Therefore, where Paul and others, addressed their letters to churches, (at that time, there weren't individual denominations.) they would have been read out to one group before being passed on to another.

Although Christians still meet in people's homes nowadays, they might well be part of a larger church. It is very rare that a whole town or city will be known as one church, and while there are splendid examples of some working together in these places, they still retain a form of individuality and denominational allegiance.

Denominations are a human development that we simply do not see in the New Testament. However, quite early on in the new church we see the beginnings of denominational principles emerging. The apostle Paul writes in his 1st letter to the Corinthian church in chapter 3 headed in some Bible versions *Divisions in the Church*:

> "You are still worldly. For since there is jealousy and quarrelling among you, are you not worldly? Are you not acting like mere humans?" (1 Corinthians 3:3)

He goes on to say:

> "For when one says, 'I follow Paul', and another, 'I follow Apollos', are you not mere human beings?" (1 Corinthians 3:4)

Here we see human influences beginning to rear their heads and affect the conduct of Christians. Yet in spite of the many thousands of denominations forming (and not being God's original intention), He does still work with them for the furtherance of His gospel.

In the light of Chapter 4, *A Wedding Planned,* I wonder whether we will eventually see the re-emergence of single named churches in towns and cities across the world?

Chapter Six

The Church in Practice

At the time of writing this book, the world is emerging from the grip of the Coronavirus pandemic that has seen the sad deaths of thousands upon thousands of people, in virtually every corner of the earth.

Many have spent weeks in hospital, many of them in intensive care wards on oxygen and ventilators, literally fighting for their lives. In communities, whole families have been isolated in their homes, in an attempt to curtail the spread of the rampant infection. This has placed intolerable strain on individuals and whole populations.

In this maelstrom of uncertainty, we have seen the church quietly rising to the challenge by providing food and other basic necessities, delivering food parcels and medicines to needy people in their locality. Also, church members have been visiting and checking on neighbours and others in the vicinity, to ensure they have at least some contacts with other human beings. There have been numerous heart-warming stories in the media of the creativity and initiatives of churches as a whole in meeting this need – setting up of food banks, formation of delivery services, meeting of social needs where feasible and much, much more.

In short, the church has been continuing the work it has been noted for down through the centuries. Many organisations and charities have their roots in Christian works of mercy, providing succour to the needy and the vulnerable members of our society, and this recent work has been a continuation of their original *raison d'être.*

In Luke 10, Jesus teaches about how He expected people to treat others. The *Parable of the Good Samaritan* is probably the most well-known of all, telling the story of a man (presumably a Jew) falling into the hands of robbers, as he travels on a road that wound through a rugged, bleak and rocky terrain. They leave him beaten and bleeding, at the mercy of whoever else might pass along the same road.

A Levite and a priest - those who should have known better and tended to him, just walked past without stopping to render aid. A Samaritan (who the Jews hated and vice-versa) comes upon the injured man and takes him to an inn where he can receive help. It is interesting to read the last words of Jesus in this parable. He concludes:

> "Which of these three do you think was a neighbour to the man who fell into the hands of robbers?" The expert in the law replied, "The one who had mercy on him." Jesus told him, "Go and do likewise." (Luke 10:36-37)

This one parable has had an immense impact on the church down through the ages and has spawned many acts and ministries of mercy towards people across the world.

Primarily, however, the church is charged with carrying out the great commission, which Jesus gave to His disciples just before He ascended into heaven. There are two recordings of this, first at the end of Matthew's gospel:

> "Then Jesus came to them and said, 'All authority in heaven and on earth has been given to me. Therefore, go and make disciples of all nations, baptizing them in the name of the Father and of the Son and of the Holy Spirit, and teaching them to obey everything I have commanded you. And surely, I am with you always, to the very end of the age.' " (Matthew 28:18-20)

The second rendering of this commission is given in greater detail at the end of Mark's gospel:

> He said to them, "Go into all the world and preach the gospel to all creation. Whoever believes and is baptized will be saved, but whoever does not believe will be condemned. And these signs will accompany those who believe: In my name they will drive out demons; they will speak in new tongues; they will pick up snakes with their hands; and when they drink deadly poison, it will not hurt them at all; they will place their hands on sick people, and they will get well." (Mark 16:15-18)

Taking both of these texts together, we get a good starting point for the work of the church. It is interesting to note how some of the elements in Mark have been filtered out over the centuries. For example, the preaching of the gospel and teachings of Jesus have been a staple part of the church, but the speaking in tongues, healing of the sick and signs, wonders and miracles have, within some denominations, ceased to be a part of the work of God.

There is of course much, much more to the work of the church than those cited above.

Across the world, in the wide variety of churches, there will be different interpretations of what the church in practice looks like. Much of this will be cultural, and to try and replicate them outside of their locales would be counter-productive. However, as we have seen in the instructions of the great commission in Matthew and Mark, there are some foundational purposes that the church should be engaged in.

Probably the mainstay of the church is that of preaching of the gospel. But, how many of today's congregations have actually examined or asked themselves what the 'gospel' means? Doubtless, it would revolve around the death and resurrection of Jesus, and yes this would be entirely correct. However, when we study the teachings of Jesus and the letters of Paul and others in the New Testament, we will find that the gospel is quite broad in its meaning and application.

When we look at how the gospel was explained to the people in the New Testament, we find that they were made aware of far more than just the death and resurrection of Jesus. For example, in Acts 8:26-40 there is the story of Philip who meets an important official of Candace, Queen of the Ethiopians. The guy is being driven along in a chariot and he is reading from the book of Isaiah. Philip hears him reading aloud, (as was the custom of that day) and engages the official in conversation. When asked what the passage from Isaiah means, Philip seizes the opportunity to tell him about Jesus.

Towards the end of this encounter, we read:

> "As they travelled along the road, they came to some water and the eunuch said, 'Look, here is water. What can stand in the way of my being baptized?' And he gave orders to stop the chariot. Then both Philip and the eunuch went down into the water and Philip baptized him". (Acts 8:36-38)

From this account we see that Philip must have talked about the significance of baptism in his telling of what we call the gospel. There are several other places where people were baptised immediately on receiving Jesus as Lord of their lives e.g., Lydia and her household (Acts 16:15) and the jailer and his family (Acts 16:33). It therefore seems that baptism was very much a part of the gospel that was preached and practiced. Interestingly, I have only once been at a baptismal service where the invitation was offered for people to give their lives to Jesus and be baptised immediately. Now I know that there are practicalities to be overcome – in particular that of having a change of clothing (and maybe the Ethiopian official had some in his chariot!) but it is noteworthy that churches do not seem to make any provision for this part of the gospel.

Gathering Together

When Jesus told His disciples that He would build His church, He wasn't referring to a building. As we have already seen, the Greek word used is *ekklesia*, which means an assembly or a gathering of people. Wherever Christians meet together, there the church exists. My wife and I were once in an airport terminal in San Francisco waiting for the final part of our journey to a Christian conference. We were surrounded by people from different parts of the USA and the world, all delayed from flying because of bad weather. It wasn't long before we discovered that we were all heading for the same conference and pretty soon we saw groups of delegates engaged in deep conversation and, in one case, praying with a person. This brought home to me just how versatile the church can and should be.

We, as the church, are not to be confined to a particular building, recognising that God gathers us together to worship Him and to be encouraged and built up. This can take place in any number of situations and locations. In the Bible we see the early church meeting together in the temple courts and in one another's homes. In several of Paul's letters he sends greetings to the church that meets in people's homes e.g., Priscilla and Aquilla (Romans 16:3-5 and 1 Corinthians 16:19), Nympha (Colossians 4:15), and Philemon (Philemon 1:2)

Churches in many countries are not able to meet openly, but have to join together secretly to avoid the possibility of discovery. In these circumstances, to be a Christian can be a dangerous life.

It's Not All Plain Sailing!

Many of Paul's letters deal with issues that occurred within the various churches: in his letter to the Galatians, Paul comes straight to the point:

> "I am astonished that you are so quickly deserting the One who called you to live in the grace of Christ and are turning to a different gospel" (Galatians 1:6)

The Jewish influence was still strong in the churches and in the book of Acts we are told of an issue the apostles had to deal with in the church in Antioch:

> "Then some of the believers who belonged to the party of the Pharisees stood up and said, 'The Gentiles must be circumcised and required to keep the law of Moses.'" (Acts 15:5)

The apostles now had to consider this requirement. Peter takes a lead in this and reasons with his fellow apostles, showing how God's grace has been poured out to all believers irrespective of their race or background. They eventually come to an agreement and send a letter to the believers at Antioch telling of the decision about this issue:

> "It seemed good to the Holy Spirit and to us not to burden you with anything beyond the following requirements: You are to abstain from food sacrificed to idols, from blood, from the meat of strangled animals and from sexual immorality. You will do well to avoid these things." (Acts 15:28-29)

It is not surprising then, that historically, there have been, such strong differences among Christians and sadly, these differences have sometimes resulted in separations within fellowships. The partings have in turn, led to the creation of new gatherings of believers, which have resulted in new denominations being formed. This has surely grieved God's heart, but because of His great grace He has worked with denominations to bring people into a saving knowledge of Himself.

Paul writes in his letter to the Philippian church:

> "It is true that some preach Christ out of envy and rivalry, but others out of goodwill. The latter do so out of love, knowing that I am put here for the defence of the gospel. The former preach Christ out of selfish ambition, not sincerely, supposing that they can stir up trouble for me while I am in chains. But what does it matter? The important thing is that in every way, whether from false motives or true, Christ is preached. And because of this I rejoice." (Philippians 1:15-18)

Paul here is saying that whatever our differences, his hope and desire is that Christ is preached to those who do not know Him personally.

The church is made up of diverse people and it is always a challenge to get everyone facing the same way. Sometimes there is separation, but as with Paul's statement above, it is hoped that Jesus is continually preached so that people might be saved.

At times, even leaders disagree and separate. Paul and Barnabas had a parting of the ways over the issue of whether they should take John Mark with them. (Barnabas and Mark were cousins). Barnabas, ever the encourager, said they should take him on their 2nd missionary journey but Paul disagreed:

> "Barnabas wanted to take John, also called Mark, with them, but Paul did not think it wise to take him, because he had deserted them in Pamphylia and had not continued with them in the work. They had such a sharp disagreement that they parted company. Barnabas took Mark and sailed for Cyprus. but Paul chose Silas and left, commended by the believers to the grace of the Lord." (Acts 15:37-40)

It is regrettable when this happens in the church, but if grace is shown by both sides and any animosity quashed, though differences may remain, the honour of Jesus is maintained. It is ironic that Barnabas, who originally brought the newly converted Saul (as he was known then) to the church, convincing them that Paul's conversion was genuine and sincere, yet they still had a falling out some time later!

Even though we might find this separation difficult to comprehend, God used both Paul and Silas, and Barnabas and Mark powerfully in their travels. Paul, after a period of time and perhaps reflection, shows His respect for both Barnabas and Mark in subsequent letters to the churches.

In 1 Corinthians 9:6 Paul who is discussing the rights of an apostle, asks the question *"is it only I and Barnabas who must work for a living?"*. This letter was written when Paul was in Ephesus on his third missionary journey, and his lack of malice indicates that there had been some form of healing of his relationship with Barnabas.

Paul also mentions Mark in his second letter to Timothy:

> "Get Mark and bring him with you for he is helpful to me in my ministry." (2 Timothy 4:11)

It is worth noting that although there was personal conflict between Paul and Barnabas, they didn't let this interfere with their work of preaching Christ. In actual fact, even though the devil may have been stirring things up between Paul and Barnabas, the end result was that the effectiveness of their missionary endeavours doubled. It appears that the way they handled the disagreement was still honouring to the Lord and He continued to work with both of them.

From the verses above we can see that even though there may be a separating of Christian brothers and sisters it doesn't have to be permanent and there can be reconciliation and restoration between them.

We could write a whole book on the practice of the church and indeed many books have been written, dealing with this subject. Across the world there are many church practices which have been born out of a necessity or a heart for the people of a particular locality.

Chapter Seven

The Church as a Body

We could have included the text of this chapter in the previous section. However, Paul refers to this metaphor of the church being like a human body in several of his letters (Ephesians 4:15-16, 5:22-23, Romans 12:4-5, 1 Corinthians 12:12-31). It would, therefore, seem prudent to devote a separate chapter to this characteristic of the church.

Paul refers to the body of Christ, using the analogy of the human body with Christ as its head:

> "…we will grow to become in every respect the mature body of Him who is the head, that is, Christ. From Him the whole body, joined and held together by every supporting ligament, grows and builds itself up in love, as each part does its work." (Ephesians 4:15-16)

His description of the church, like parts of a human body and how they relate to each of the others, give us a very practical application about how we ought to conduct ourselves towards fellow believers.

Not only this, but verses in Ephesians above and 1 Corinthians 12:12-27, give the reasoning for Paul's instruction, namely that we all stand or fall together. There would seem to be very little or no place for individualism which we see sadly rearing its head in so many, if not all our churches today.

Paul's teaching is very much in contrast to today's western civilisation where by and large we are to make our own way in life. If it means trampling over others to achieve that end, then this is part of what we have to experience to make our way through society.

The Church as a Body

One Body, Many Parts

This is the heading given in the NIV to 1 Corinthians 12:12 – 31 (Paul makes a similar comment in Romans 12: 4-5) and provides a good starting point in our discussion. Whether Paul had any specific medical knowledge or awareness of the human body or was just writing from his general awareness of it, we do not know, but the parts he brings to the reader's attention give a good understanding of the spiritual application he needs to convey.

We see in these texts a brilliant correlation that leaves the reader in no doubt as to the importance of how we relate to one another in the church. While Paul had to overcome the prejudices between Jews and Gentile that were so prevalent in his day, we still see this in our own developed society.

He further emphasises that we need one another. No-one is more important than the other (even leaders in the church, though this is not mentioned here). In fact, it would leave us feeling somewhat foolish to think that one part e.g., eye or ear, hand or foot, is more significant that someone else.

Paul ties in his argument with previous points on spiritual gifts earlier in 1 Corinthians 12. The analogy regarding the body serves to underline that, no matter what gifting a person might have, all have equal importance and relevance in the body of the church.

It is, sadly, a human trait that we consciously or unconsciously highlight the importance of our gifts and abilities according to the place they take in society. While some may appear to be more necessary than others, for example, medical or emergency service works over say, gardening or decorating skills, each do have a place according to when and how we have need of them. This in turn spills over into the church scenario, with greater focus given to certain spiritual gifts being of more importance than another.

Although there might appear to be scriptural evidence for this e.g., 1 Corinthians 12:31 where Paul encourages the reader to *eagerly desire the greater gifts* and 1 Corinthians 14:12 *Since you are eager for gifts of the Spirit, try to excel in those that build up the church,* he is not speaking about a hierarchy of giftings. He is more concerned with the effect in people's lives and on the church itself. The emphasis of Paul's teaching in 1 Corinthians 12 is, as the sub-title in NIV says, that there is only one body, but that it is made up of many diverse parts, each having their own place and function that contributes to the whole.

The amazing feature about this teaching is that it has local, trans-local, national and global application; such is the breadth and scope of Jesus' church. However, primarily, this teaching would apply to the local gathering of God's people, for there it is principally worked out. If this concept is grasped at a local level, then it will permeate across the whole of the body of Christ.

When the members of the body are functioning as God intends; it grows:

> "the whole body, joined and held together by every joint with which it is equipped, when each part is working properly, makes the body grow so that it builds itself up in love." (Ephesians 4:16 - English Standard Version)

This body, just like our human bodies needs food (the word of God – Matthew 4:4) and water (the work of the Holy Spirit – John 7:37-38) and we have a responsibility to ensure we eat and drink every day if we are to continue to function as God intended. We have to look after the body and in the verses of 1 Corinthians 12:12-27 we see this mutual care aspect being emphasised. The telling phrase, *if one part suffers, every part suffers with it; if one part is honoured, every part rejoices with it* (v26) shows us that the body of Christ is one of caring and identifying with each member of the body. This sets the church above every other organisation across the world. I have seen it personally coming into play at conferences and other gatherings where there has been a mixing of people from across different nations. Christ has joined us together like no other group of people.

The Church as the Body of Christ

In several scriptures we are told that Christ is the head of the body which is the church, (Ephesians 1:22, 4:15, Colossians 1:18, 2:19), and He directs, guides and generally influences it. This headship is the authority that He has in our lives and over the body of the church. He is the supreme ruler and creator as Colossians 1:15-20 (titled *The Supremacy of Christ* in the NIV)

Christ is allowed to affect all that we do and say when we submit our lives to Him *and* to His rule. The model however, sadly falls down when we step out from under His headship and desire to go our own way or choose to disobey the guidance of scripture.

Jesus doesn't force His headship upon us. His is a loving leadership which only works effectively when we in turn lovingly follow Him. It should be our desire to *want* Him to be head over us and so to please Him. Just as in a loving marriage, where each partner desires to please the other and give himself or herself to each one, so it is with the members of the body, the church. As we have seen earlier in Ephesians 4:16, the body *grows and builds itself up in love* the very succinct note that *each part does its work*.

The Greek rendering of this verse reads:

> "The increase of the body makes for itself to [the] building up of itself in love"[10]

Paul is saying that the body of Christ – the church, increases or grows when it builds itself up in love in all areas not just numerically. With Christ as the head, He is both the goal and the source of the Church's growth. The love of Christ as head of the church flows into the church, bringing growth, and that love flows back towards the head as a result of what the church has received.

---

[10] www.biblehub.com/ephesians/4-16.htm Greek rendering of Eph 4:16

When we look at the church as body corporate, our individual decisions fade into the background and the actuality of Jesus as head comes to the fore.

Unlike the human body, which cannot function at all unless the brain (head) tells it what to do, each member of the body of Christ has the choice to follow His directions or to go in a direction of our own choice.

Following His triumph on the Cross where He defeated all His enemies and even death itself, Jesus is now head over everything:

> "…in Christ you have been brought to fullness. He is the head over every power and authority." (Colossians 2:10)

This headship now governs all that happens throughout the universe, for all things have been placed beneath His feet (1 Corinthians 15:27, Ephesians 1:22) and as such He has the pre-eminence over all.

Our loving response follows His written guidance in the Bible and His voice speaking to us in the many different ways that He does.

Once we give our lives to Him through salvation, we become knitted and joined with Him. We then become part of the church, which is His body, representing Him here on earth. We should be living our lives as if Jesus was still physically with us. We are the representation of Jesus in this world. The Church is the organism through which Christ manifests His life to the world today.

Unlike a human body, which once born, ceases to grow new parts, the body of Christ, the church, continues to have new parts or members grafted on.

A body can refer to an individual or it can refer to a group - the church. Whilst we can think of the body of Christ in an individualistic sense, we also have to think in terms of a number of people making up the body. Therefore, when we think of the church as the body of Christ, we ought also to think of it as being comprised of a great number of individual persons.

The Church as a Body

Once a human being reaches the age of around 21 our bodies generally stop growing, although there are some individual parts that continue to grow slightly. The body of Christ never stops growing. There is always room for new members to be joined to the main body and in this sense the body of Christ is continually growing and expanding. This is the glorious feature of Jesus church; there is always capacity for more to be added to the body of Christ.

Chapter Eight

The Work of the Holy Spirit

It was John the Baptist who first introduced the new era of the Holy Spirit's work within us when he proclaimed:

> "I baptize you with water for repentance. But after me comes One who is more powerful than I, whose sandals I am not worthy to carry. He will baptize you with the Holy Spirit and fire."
> (Matthew 3:11)

The word 'baptise' that John uses here means to dip repeatedly, to immerse or submerge. This is what John was doing in the river Jordan – people were receiving a baptism of repentance. Luke's Gospel gives greater detail of what this means, where John the Baptist teaches about living a different way of life. (Luke 3:1-14)

It is in this context of being immersed, that John, led by the Spirit, tells them that Jesus would baptise with the Holy Spirit and with fire.

For us as Christians, it is Jesus whom we look to as our role model and guide. In examining the work of the Holy Spirit, we look to Jesus example and direction.

We see at His baptism, that the Holy Spirit descended on Him in the form of a dove. The apostle John in his gospel says:

> Then John gave this testimony: "I saw the Spirit come down from heaven as a dove and remain on Him. And I myself did not know Him, but the one who sent me to baptize with water told me, 'The man on whom you see the Spirit come down and remain, is the one who will baptize with the Holy Spirit.' I have seen and I testify that this is God's Chosen One."
> (John 1:32-34)

Isaiah also says about Jesus in his prophecy:

> "The Spirit of the Sovereign LORD is on me, because the LORD has anointed me to preach good news to the poor." (Isaiah 61:1)

Jesus later confirms when reading this prophecy in a synagogue:

> "Today this scripture is fulfilled in your hearing." (Luke 4:21)

I find it interesting to note that after His baptism, Jesus is recorded as being *full* of the Holy Spirit and then *led* by the Spirit into the wilderness (Luke 4:1). Then in v14 He is reported as returning in the *power* of the Holy Spirit. It would appear to me then, that Jesus, although fully God, was dependent on the working of the Holy Spirit in Him to carry out His earthly mission. Jesus came to earth partly to be an example to us of how we can and should be led by the Holy Spirit in our day-to-day lives. If God considered it necessary for Jesus to be baptised and filled with the Holy Spirit, then surely shouldn't we also follow His example?

Instead, we have a division within the church. On one side, we have those who believe that the baptism of the Spirit is still very much a part of today's church. On the other hand, there are those who say that the baptism isn't for today because the Holy Spirit is within us once we accept Jesus as Lord of our lives and there is no further need for additional experience of Him.

Some of the argument against the baptism of the Holy Spirit is because this encounter with the Spirit has been misused in the church by ill-informed or over enthusiastic leaders, putting people off from having anything to do with Him.

The events of Pentecost recorded in Acts 2 are the commissioning of the church. They are the beginning of the fulfilment of the Isaiah 61 prophecy and although primarily this refers to the work of Jesus, it is by implication and association, the ongoing work of the church. I say beginning of the fulfilment, because it is still continuing - every believer who asks for and receives the Holy Spirit is baptised (or filled) with the Holy Spirit.

On two occasions Jesus foretold the events of Pentecost and instructed the disciples to expect this to happen. We aren't given any indications about the questions they might have had about when this would happen. Irrespective of any reservations on their part, the Holy Spirit was poured out on all the believers gathered there.

When the Holy Spirit literally rains down on the 120 believers and they start speaking in tongues (other languages) Peter is given the interpretation by the Holy Spirit of what is happening, namely, fulfilment of the prophecy given by the prophet Joel and Peter says:

> "Repent and be baptized, every one of you, in the name of Jesus Christ for the forgiveness of your sins. And you will receive the gift of the Holy Spirit. The promise is for you and your children and for all who are far off - for all whom the Lord our God will call." (Acts 2:38-39)

Peter is saying that what has happened to these believers can also happen to those subsequently coming to faith in Christ. Note he says the Holy Spirit is a gift – a personal gift for believers.

Now the Holy Spirit is a person, just as God the Father is a person and God the Son is a person. The Holy Spirit is the third person of the Trinity of God.

Why was He given to the believers? Jesus had already taught His disciples about the Holy Spirit and the work He would do beforehand in preparation for this moment in the commission of their ministry.

In John 14:15-31, Jesus interestingly gives them a 'heads-up':

> "I have told you now before it happens, so that when it does happen you will believe." (John 14:29)

Jesus introduces the Holy Spirit as the Counsellor, (also known as the advocate or helper) saying that He would be with them forever. He also tells them:

The Work of the Holy Spirit

> "But the Advocate, the Holy Spirit, whom the Father will send in my name, will teach you all things and will remind you of everything I have said to you." (John 14:26)

So then, Jesus is leaving nothing to chance. He (and the Father) knows how easily humans can forget things so the Holy Spirit is sent to bear witness to what Jesus has taught them. Thus, the Holy Spirit brought to their minds all the words of Jesus. Remember that at that time there wasn't anything written down – at least not officially - of what Jesus said. Now we have the benefit of the New Testament which records the teachings of Jesus.

It is interesting to note that when Jesus tells the disciples to wait in Jerusalem for the promised Holy Spirit, He also tells them:

> "But you will receive power when the Holy Spirit comes on you; and you will be my witnesses in Jerusalem, and in all Judea and Samaria, and to the ends of the earth." (Acts 1:8)

The word 'power' used here is *dynamis*[11] in the Greek and means power, mighty work, strength, miracle, might. As we see later in the book of Acts, the disciples are now transformed from cowering, fearful men to bold witnesses for Jesus. And this is what the Holy Spirit is still doing in the lives of men and women who are baptised in or with the Holy Spirit today.

The principal reason for being baptised in the Holy Spirit is to be given the power to carry out the work of being called to Christ. As I have already said, Jesus came from the desert in the *power* of the Holy Spirit after His trial of being tempted (Luke 4:14). I am not suggesting that to move in the power of the Holy Spirit, we have to undergo a period of similar testing. However, we do need the filling of the Holy Spirit, so that we might have power to accomplish all that we are called to do. Jesus knew the disciples needed this infilling or baptism of the Holy Spirit; do we then need any less?

---

[11] Strong's Exhaustive Concordance – dynamis G1411

We see this power of the Holy Spirit being with Jesus on specific occasions, for example:

> All the people were amazed and said to each other, "What words these are! With authority and power, He gives orders to impure spirits and they come out!" (Luke 4:36)

It seems that Luke is given understanding regarding this power of the Holy Spirit as he mentions it several times.

- the **power** of the Lord was with Jesus to heal the sick, (5:17)
- the people all tried to touch Him, because **power** was coming from Him and healing them all, (6:19)
- (regarding the woman subject to bleeding for twelve years), Jesus said, "Someone touched me; I know that **power** has gone out from me" (8:46 - my insertion)

During Jesus' ministry it would appear that this power of the Holy Spirit was transferrable. When Jesus sent out the disciples, on their first mission it is recorded that Jesus:

> gave them **power** and authority to drive out all demons and to cure diseases. (Luke 9:1)

Jesus later prepares the disciples for life without Him physically in their midst by telling them:

> "I am going to send you what my Father has promised; but stay in the city until you have been clothed with power from on high." (Luke 24:49)

And He reiterates this in His final instructions in Acts 8:1 before ascending to heaven.

Each of these renderings of the word *power* is the same Greek word, having the same meaning namely, strength, power or ability.

There is also evidence that points to the need for further filling of the Holy Spirit. John records that when the disciples were together with doors locked for fear of the Jews (John 20:19). Jesus appears in the room and says:

> "Peace be with you! As the Father has sent me, I am sending you." And with that He breathed on them and said, "Receive the Holy Spirit." (John 20:21-22)

Then there is the mighty outpouring of the Holy Spirit at Pentecost, followed by yet another filling of the Spirit after a prayer meeting (Acts 4:31). There are further occurrences of this, which point to the fact that this filling of the Holy Spirit is an ongoing process.

The apostle Paul writes:

> "Do not get drunk on wine, which leads to debauchery. Instead, be filled with the Spirit." (Ephesians 5:18)

The phrase 'be filled with the Holy Spirit' is a Greek present imperative tense, which means in essence *'to go on being filled'*. Why do we need to go on being filled with the Holy Spirit? Some caustically or glibly ask "Do we leak the Holy Spirit"? as if we are some sort of vessel that has a hole in it? This is not the case at all but being continuously filled with the Holy Spirit keeps us on top of our game so to speak. It ensures that we are in step with Him in our walk with Jesus. In the context that Paul writes these words, he is cautioning against too much alcohol, which deadens our senses and causes us to become lax in our behaviour. If we think back to the setting of Pentecost, the disciples were accused of being drunk, but Peter reminds those accusers that it was only 9.00 in the morning – in essence saying, "the pubs aren't even open yet!"

The giving of the Holy Spirit is to fill us with the power of God so that we can be effective witnesses for Him in bringing the gospel to the world around us, not only with words but also with action e.g., signs, wonders and miracles.

I remember at one time thinking through this text (probably as I was preparing to preach and needed to include this text) when God showed me a balloon that was being inflated. At any stage of the inflation, it can be said that the balloon is full of air. Yet as we continue to inflate the balloon, it grows and expands. God was showing me that as we continue to ask to be filled with the Holy Spirit, He is in fact *expanding* our capacity for the work He has for us to do.

The Holy Spirit bears witness in our hearts that when we hear the gospel and teachings about the Christian faith we can believe and accept them. He also enables us to understand and believe in the first place the message of salvation in Jesus. This is foreign to our spirits until the Holy Spirit brings illumination to our hearts and minds. Paul puts it like this:

> "When you were dead in your sins and in the uncircumcision of your flesh, God made you alive with Christ."
> (Colossians 2:13)

That is, the Holy Spirit works within us literally to give us new spiritual birth.

However, there does appear to be sufficient evidence in the scriptures to point to a work of the Spirit in coming upon us or within us in an even greater degree.

In Acts there is the account of Paul arriving in Ephesus and finding some believers:

> While Apollos was at Corinth, Paul took the road through the interior and arrived at Ephesus. There he found some disciples and asked them, "Did you receive the Holy Spirit when you believed?" They answered, "No, we have not even heard that there is a Holy Spirit." So, Paul asked, "Then what baptism did you receive?" "John's baptism," they replied. Paul said, "John's baptism was a baptism of repentance. He told the people to believe in the one coming after him, that is, in Jesus." On hearing this, they were baptized in the name of the Lord Jesus. When Paul placed his hands on them, the Holy Spirit came on them, and they spoke in tongues and prophesied.
> (Acts 19:1-6)

It is noteworthy that Paul specifically asks if they have received the Holy Spirit. First this indicates that the filling of the Holy Spirit isn't an automatic work by Him and requires our asking, and secondly, it indicates the importance we should place on the filling or baptism of the Holy Spirit.

The Holy Spirit does not force us to do anything, rather He works alongside us. He gives us gifts and abilities to do the work each one of us has been called to do, very often enhancing skills or capabilities which we already have. For example, a great many church leaders and teachers of scripture have been trained as teachers and have experience of teaching in schools and colleges. The Holy Spirit then gives them the ability to interpret and teach scripture.

However, there are times when the Holy Spirit brings about a complete change in our lives. The disciples are recorded as being in a room with the doors locked for fear of the Jews (John 20:19). Yet at Pentecost when the Holy Spirit is given, they are radically transformed, so much so, that not long after, when Peter and John are brought before the Jewish leaders after healing a disabled man at the Temple gate, the leaders take note of their courage (Acts 4:13). Additionally, when Peter and John return to the other believers and tell of their experience, the whole room bursts into a spontaneous prayer meeting where they pray for even more boldness. (Acts 4:29)

Peter, when preaching at Pentecost, spoke about the Holy Spirit being a gift that has been given from God (Acts 2:38). There are many gifts that God has given us – not only salvation, but also the ongoing work of the Holy Spirit within us.

In several places in the New Testament, the writers speak of the various gifts of the Holy Spirit. These gifts enable the Christian believer to be effective in the work of God. There are two main passages that speak about the gifts – Romans 12:6-8 and in more detail in 1 Corinthians 12:1-11. There are also gifts of ministry laid out in Ephesians 4:11.

If you do an internet search on the gifts of the Holy Spirit you will find a variety of insights about these gifts, with the number of gifts ranging from 7-19 (in one book I have read there are 21 gifts which include the gift of marriage and the gift of singleness.)

The point to highlight here is that each list that Paul gives in the above scriptures aren't all the same (the only one that is common to each is that of prophecy/prophet). I have come to understand that the gifts listed in the verses mentioned are an example of the diversity of the gifts that we can be given. The lists are not absolute as many would contend.

I have seen in churches that those who lead worship have a particular gifting. Those who are enabled to pray for many hours have the gift of intercession and so we could go on. The point I want to draw out here is that the gifts are given by the Holy Spirit and Jesus to enable us to be more effective in our witness and work for God.

Chapter Nine

Breadboard, Breadcrumbs or Fresh Bread?

There is just something about the smell of freshly baked bread that grabs our attention. If you walk past a baker's shop in the High Street where you live, the aroma of fresh bread emanating from the open door awakens our gastric juices and just cries out, "Buy me, buy me".

Perhaps there's a supermarket you use that bakes its own bread that can have the same affect. You may be one who bakes your own bread at home. As it comes out of the oven, there is an almost irresistible urge to cut a slice and savour its delicious warmth and taste.

Watching a game show on television one Saturday night, a question to a contestant was, "In a survey about house buying, which of these aromas was said to most influence those viewing a house for sale – fresh coffee, fresh linen, freshly baked bread or freshly mown grass?" I said it was fresh coffee, but in actual fact the correct answer was the smell of freshly baked bread! There's just something about the smell of it that draws us towards it.

As the church has emerged from the Covid restrictions, I recently heard someone say that they didn't want stale bread anymore, they wanted fresh bread. I thought that this was quite telling.

As I said in the previous chapter, the UK restrictions of movement put into place in March 2020 have highlighted how stale church services and our walk with God have become.

In the Bible, bread has a particular significance both in the Old and New Testaments. It was a staple part of their diet. People can survive a long time on only bread and water. At one time Jesus declared,

> "I am the bread of life. Whoever comes to me will never go hungry, and whoever believes in me will never be thirsty." (John 6:35)

By this He meant that in the same way that bread and water are essential for physical life so He is essential for our spiritual lives.

The Communion is often referred to as Breaking of Bread. It represents the Last Supper where Jesus broke the bread and gave it to His disciples, telling them that this was His body which was to be broken for them.

In the Old Testament, as part of the interior layout of the Tabernacle (and later the Temple), twelve loaves of freshly baked bread were laid out on the altar, one loaf for each of the twelve tribes of Israel. (Leviticus 24:5-9)

The bread was changed on a regular basis so that it remained fresh. It was called the 'Bread of Presence' or 'Shew Bread', and signified both the Presence and provision of God for His people. Someone has said the shew bread could be called the 'show-up' bread because God is present where the bread is.

In thinking about this subject of the presence of God my thoughts have been directed towards God's presence, both in our churches and with us as individuals. Do we experience the presence of God when we gather in our church groups, whether this be in a purpose-built church building, a converted cinema or other structure, or even our homes?

Now I know we can say that God is present everywhere at all times as He is omnipresent, yet He may not be revealed in the same way at the same time to people everywhere.

It would appear that there is now a yearning for more of the 'felt' presence of God. By this they mean an awareness of God's presence when we gather together as God's people, the 'weighty' presence of God, the '*kabod*' of God.

Why is this important? Let's look in more detail at the three parts of the title of this chapter.

Breadboard

In my house, we have a wooden breadboard, which has knife marks on it where we have previously cut our bread. It shows that at some time in the past there has been bread on this board but now all that is left are the marks of what once was.

Sadly, in many of our churches, all that is left now are the marks of what once was. There may be a plaque on the wall denoting some occasion when God moved among the people of that church, but the presence of God has long since gone.

The book of Ruth in the Old Testament is a wonderful story of tragedy and triumph, of love and joy born out of hopelessness and heartache. The story opens with a heart-breaking account of a couple, Elimelech and his wife Naomi and their two small sons having to become refugees in a foreign country because there was a famine in their own land.

We are seeing similar occurrences across many parts of the world, whether it be as a result of famine or because of war or other displacements.

It is ironic that Bethlehem, the town where Elimelech and Naomi lived, meant 'House of Bread'. But now there was no bread in the house of bread! There weren't even any breadcrumbs left, such was the severity of the famine. Elimelech and his family were left with no option other than to flee to another country.

This lack of bread can be a graphic picture of the state of many of our churches up and down the country where across the board attendances have steadily decreased for decades. There may be many factors affecting this decrease, but surely one of the main reasons is that people are not being given the opportunity to experience the fresh presence of God in the meetings.

One Sunday, I was speaking to a Baptist church pastor about how people are not coming back to church now that the Covid restrictions are being gradually lifted. He said that they were encountering the same problem as I had been hearing from other people, that the church has to change and cannot continue as it has done.

Breadcrumbs

Breadcrumbs can represent us harking back to the good old days when God moved in such and such a way. We still long for those days, yet lose sight of what God wants to do today, or even worse fail to ask Him what He wants to do in His church.

Any sense of change is met with much opposition as if it is an affront or offence to God. The implication is that if it works OK so far, then it must be fine for the foreseeable future.

Yet as DL Moody, an American evangelist who held great evangelistic campaigns and rallies in the late 1800's and early 1900's said, "God is moving on – I must keep up with Him." We have to realise that God's direction is forward and we cannot exist on the breadcrumbs of the past.

I myself have been guilty of this. In the mid 1990's there was a world-wide move of the Holy Spirit that brought much refreshing to churches that accepted it, with many coming into a new experience of the work of the Holy Spirit.

Church was fun and exciting – it wasn't to be missed. We never knew quite what God was going to do from one service to the next. I know many found this unnerving and could not cope with the unexpected, yet for myself and many others, we found this brought a freshness to the otherwise stale church format of yesteryear.

Bringing in new songbooks or overhead projection or other changes in worship doesn't rekindle what the Holy Spirit brought back then.

I have longed for those mid 1990 days again, but recently I have come to realise that they are gone now and cannot be repeated. The breadcrumbs left over from those days cannot give us enough for what we need now. We have to experience the fresh bread of the presence of God for today.

So, what do I mean when I refer to the felt presence of God, be it in our churches, homes or elsewhere? One definition I read recently describes the presence of God in this way – it's as if God Himself had walked into the room.

In the Tabernacle (and later the Temple) there was an area screened off by a thick purple curtain. Beyond this was the Holy of Holies in which God's presence dwelt. No one was allowed to enter this area except the high priest and he only entered it once a year on the day of Atonement to offer sacrifices for the people's sins.

Preparations for this day were minute and exact and any deviation from them could result in the death of the high priest. It is said that the high priest had a rope tied to him so that should he die before God, his body could be retrieved. While this is not recorded anywhere in scripture, it may have been a practical consideration – a sort of 'what if?'

There is a weightiness to God's presence – a tangible change in the atmosphere in a place. This presence of God can also be felt in the open, away from any building. There have been stories during times of revival when people have been so overcome by the presence of God in fields or on roads; they have to stop what they are doing and call on God's mercy. When His presence convicted men and women of their sin, they had to get their lives right with Him there and then.

This presence can effect changes in people's lives without any human intervention. We are told in Acts 5:15 that people brought sick people onto the streets so that Peter's shadow might fall on them and bring about their healing. There was nothing special about Peter's shadow in and of itself, but it was the presence of God with Him, that drew them to Him and brought the healing of people.

In Matthew 14:36-37 we read that people brought their sick to Jesus and begged Him to let them touch the hem of His robe so that they might be healed. Several of the Gospels carry the account of the woman subject to bleeding for 12 years. When she touched the hem of Jesus' garment she was cured and Jesus felt power go out of Him. Yes, this was faith on her part, but it was also the presence of God with Jesus that enabled her to be healed without Him saying anything to her or reaching out His hand to touch her.

There is a story about the great revivalist Charles Finney who was once travelling on a train. As he passed through a small town of Houghton, New York state, people were convicted of their sin and fell on their knees crying out to God for forgiveness.

And there are many others who through history have carried the presence of God and affected those around them.

Fresh Bread

Returning to our story from the book of Ruth; after a long time, Naomi's sons have grown up, married but sadly along with her husband Elimelech, have died. Word gets back to Naomi that the Lord had come to the aid of His people and that there is food once again in the land – effectively there is now bread in the house. Naomi sets off back to her homeland, with one of her daughters-in-law, Ruth travelling with her.

Word gets round quickly when God is present in a place. A few years ago, word filtered through that there had been a significant move of God in a church in Cwmbran in Wales. So, one Saturday afternoon, two car loads of people from the church I attended drove over to experience this for ourselves.

People want to be where God is present and is moving among them. This is what is experienced during times of revival. Large numbers of people are drawn by the Holy Spirit to those places where God is present, and even though it means some distress in getting their lives right with God, yet more and more people are drawn.

Nowadays, with the ease of international air travel, this happens at a considerable rate. In no time at all it seems, people arrive from across various parts of the world to experience the presence of God, for that in reality is what Christians want.

Leonard Ravenhill, an English pastor and revivalist who emigrated to America in the 1950's made this statement, "The church has become so sub-normal, that were it to become normal, it would be viewed as abnormal." This is indeed a telling statement and could be a chapter all of its own, but it does underpin this matter of a lack of fresh bread in God's house. So, what are we to do to usher in the tangible, felt presence of God – the fresh bread of His presence?

In the Old Testament there were several kings who sought to do what was right in the eyes of God. One of these, Josiah, became king when he was eight years old – we read this account in 2 Kings 22:1 – 23:30

When he was twenty-six, Josiah started re-establishing God's ordinances in the kingdom of Judah, in particular the restoration work of the temple. During this work the book of the Law was found. It was read to King Josiah, who on hearing its contents tore his robes (a sign of distress and repentance toward God) and ordered that the commands of God and His ordinances be re-established in the land. As a result, Josiah made a covenant with God to follow the Lord and keep His commands, regulations and decrees with all his heart and all his soul. The people also pledged themselves to the covenant.

There were other kings who also carried out similar acts before God, but it is recorded about Josiah:

> "Neither before nor after Josiah was there a king like him who turned to the LORD as he did—with all his heart and with all his soul and with all his strength, in accordance with all the Law of Moses." (2 Kings 23:25)

Therefore, it would seem to me that there has to be some radical actions taken within the church to rouse the people of God to return to Him with all their heart and minds. We have to return, not to the book of the Law in the Old Testament but to Jesus' teachings and the acts of the early church. There we see God working in a new way among His people - that is moving away from the Old Testament ways with its rituals and ordinances.

Josiah repaired the temple and He stopped all the foreign practices that had crept in which were offensive to God. In short, Josiah carried out a massive root and branch clear out and re-established God's holy commands. This probably caused a disagreement with those who benefited from them, but such was Josiah's determination to go back to God's commands that he wasn't swayed by the opposition.

I've heard of one church leader who believed God was saying to close down the satellite locations of his church and go back to their roots. He said it was painful, but it was better to experience it then rather than face God at the judgement time.

I believe that the church has to go though some painful, root and branch changes and ask God how He wants His people to look for the future. This will not be easy and there may be some who disagree with actions that are taken, but we have to realise afresh that this is not our church – it belongs to Jesus. He endured the agonies of the Cross and died so that the church could be established.

As Jesus told His disciples:

> "*I* will build *My* church and the gates of hades will not stand against it". (Matthew 16:18 – my emphasis)

Today it may seem that more than ever the gates of hell itself are standing against Jesus' church, but we have to have confidence that Jesus will triumph over all that stands against Him.

Are we hearing what God is saying at this time or will we just pick up where we left off in early 2020? Jesus wants His church back and will take the action necessary to accomplish this.

We could surely say, He would not do anything drastic or dramatic? Tell that to those who've been through the heartbreak of seeing a church close - years of labouring for God, only to see their struggles go down the drain. Tell that to those who have seen a church building that once rang with praises to God now being used as a theatre or restaurant or other use. There is one such church, now being used as a restaurant in West Street, Chichester, West Sussex. I've sat in that place and looked around and felt a sadness, wondering what happened to it. What heartache the members went through as they saw the work dwindle to such a point that it had to stop.

God does allow churches to close down. As incomprehensible as this may seem, it has sadly happened, and will continue to do so in the future.

Chapter 10

Grasping the Horns of the Altar

Where are the prayer warriors who storm heaven's gates and the throne-room of God, imploring Him for more of His power in the life of the church? Yes, I understand they will be found in the secret place – the prayer closets or war rooms (if you have ever seen the film War Room, you will know what I mean.) There is a place for passionate, corporate, public prayer. But sadly, the enemy has lulled vast sections of the church to sleep. Prayer meetings are poorly attended, with little or no emphasis on the importance of prayer. If people do not pray for their church, who will?

The parable of the persistent widow in Luke's gospel, graphically demonstrates Jesus' attitude to prayer,

> "Then Jesus told His disciples a parable to show them that they should always pray and not give up." (Luke 18:1)

The church seems to have given up seeking God for His presence within its activities. What a contrast with the church described in Acts. When Peter and John returned from their interrogation before the Sanhedrin after healing the disabled man at the Temple gate, did the church say, "Oh well, we'd better not do anything like this (healing people) so that we do not upset the authorities or get ourselves into trouble?" Not at all!

> "Now, Lord, consider their (the Sanhedrin) threats and enable Your servants to speak Your word with great boldness. Stretch out Your hand to heal and perform signs and wonders through the name of Your holy servant Jesus".
> (Acts 4:29-30 - my insertion)

The church as we would say were 'spitting tin-tacks'! They saw the Sanhedrin's attempts to silence them as an affront to Jesus' commands and prayed that God would do something about it. They did not have to wait long for His answer:

> "After they prayed, the place where they were meeting was shaken. And they were all filled with the Holy Spirit and spoke the word of God boldly." (Acts 4:31)

God's answer to their prayers was swift in coming. Their will lined up with God's will, producing, literally, a ground-shaking encounter! Oh, that we would have prayer meetings like this, with people who know how to shake the very bars and gates of heaven until God answers.

Moses wasn't afraid to do this before God:

> "Then Moses said to Him, 'If Your Presence does not go with us, do not send us up from here. How will anyone know that You are pleased with me and with Your people unless You go with us? What else will distinguish me and Your people from all the other people on the face of the earth?' "
> (Exodus 33:15-16)

In today's church we would perhaps say, "Well, we can't say anything like that to God. It would be rude and an affront to Him. It certainly would not be a very politically correct approach."

But what was God's answer to Moses? Did He strike him down with some deadly disease or severely reprimand or rebuke him for his rudeness?

> "And the LORD said to Moses, 'I will do the very thing you have asked, because I am pleased with you and I know you by name.' " (Exodus 33:17)

What we think is rudeness and improper before God and what He thinks is unacceptable are two very different issues. Yes, we do come before a Holy God and we approach Him with reverence and holy fear, but from accounts that we read in the Bible it would appear that God welcomes boldness and actually commends people who demonstrate that before Him.

> "Let us therefore come boldly to the throne of grace, that we may obtain mercy and find grace to help in time of need." (Hebrews 4:16 - New King James version)

Grasping the Horns of the Altar

After writing the text above and thinking about it later in the day the phrase, *'grasping the horns of the altar'* came into my mind. It had to be a prompting from God through the Holy Spirit as it's not something that I would readily think about! So, I did a bit of research and found two occasions where someone grasped the horns of the altar.

In the Tabernacle and Temple layout there were two altars – one for the burnt sacrifices and one for the offering of incense. The altar for burnt sacrifices was the larger of the two and was placed in the outer court. The Altar of Incense was a lot smaller and was placed just in front of the veil or curtain that separated the Holy Place from the Holy of Holies (or Most Holy place) containing the Ark of the covenant.

God had given instructions to Moses about the altar being a place of refuge under certain circumstances:

> "Anyone who strikes a person with a fatal blow is to be put to death. However, if it is not done intentionally but God lets it happen, they are to flee to a place I will designate. 'But if anyone schemes and kills someone deliberately, that person is to be taken from My altar and put to death.'"
> (Exodus 21:12-14)

The two people recorded as having grasped the horns of the altar (the altar of burnt offering), fled to it for safety. They were Joab and Adonijah who conspired together to put Adonijah on the throne after his father, King David's death.

So, what is the significance of this phrase *grasping the horns of the altar* for the church today? We are no longer bound by the Old Covenant, so God must have brought this expression to my mind with a New Covenant implication.

The altars were a place where God and humans met. They were places of exchange, communication, and influence. God had left specific instructions regarding the altar:

> "The fire must be kept burning on the altar continuously; it must not go out." (Leviticus 6:13)

Prayer is like the altar – it must be kept going continuously and with passion. I believe that God is speaking to us with regard to this aspect of our praying. If we look back at the prayer of the church in Acts 4:29-31 we can get a flavour of their passion in the church at that time.

While in the Old Testament the altar was designated as a place of safety, I believe that this indicates the need for the church to fall on God for His mercy and help with a passion and determination.

Grasping hold of the hem of His garment also lines up with a similar image of desperation but also determination. The woman subject to bleeding for twelve years is recorded as saying:

> "If I only touch His cloak, I will be healed." (Matthew 9:21)

There is the same connection with going to God for safety and healing. Jesus did not rebuke the woman for her apparent affrontery in approaching Him. Under Jewish law she shouldn't even have been out in public, let alone approaching a religious teacher, albeit quietly and unobtrusively.

When we approach God in prayer, especially in a way we would deem to be offensive or with a sense of affrontery, (as we saw with Moses above), it would appear that God welcomes it. Why is this?

God sees (as with Moses) that what is driving a person is the heart that is right before Him. This is also evident when Samuel was tasked by God with choosing the next king to succeed Saul:

> "The Lord does not look at the things people look at. People look at the outward appearance, but the LORD looks at the heart." (1 Samuel 16:7)

For the New Testament church, the altar of burnt offering represents the sacrifice that Jesus became for each one of us. Hebrews 7:27 tells us that *Jesus sacrificed once for all* so that there is no longer any need for the sacrifice of animals.

So, in grasping the horns of the altar, we recognise the massive debt we owe to Jesus in His offering Himself in our place. We mentally and spiritually grab hold of the sacrifice of Jesus. In doing so we also recognise our deep need for His help and intervention in the situations in which we find ourselves. Yes, at times we do go to Him in desperation, recognising there is nothing else we can do and there is no-one else who can help us. Even when we go to Him in the first instance, we may recognise that we desperately need His intervention.

Twice the writer to the Hebrews exhorts about the manner in which we should approach God:

> "Let us then approach God's throne of grace with confidence, so that we may receive mercy and find grace to help us in our time of need." (Hebrews 4:16)

> "Therefore, brothers and sisters, since we have confidence to enter the Most Holy Place by the blood of Jesus, by a new and living way opened for us through the curtain, that is, His body, and since we have a great priest over the house of God, let us draw near to God with a sincere heart and with the full, assurance that faith brings," (Hebrews 10:19-22)

For each of these pericopes we might feel somewhat uneasy in approaching God. We have been taught that He is so holy that He is virtually unapproachable. Then, if we do so it should be in hushed tones and with a Uriah Heep (with a cloying humility) attitude. Yet when we read these verses and of how David and the other contributors to the Psalms came before Him, we should be reassured that God accepts boldness and confidence.

The Man who Wrestled with God

Jacob, (who was to be later renamed Israel – the father of the Israelite nation), was a schemer, a scoundrel and a swindler. If there was a fast buck to be made or an advantage to be gained over someone else, Jacob was your man. He fleeced (excuse the pun!) everyone, including his brother, Esau and his uncle Laban. When the brothers were young men, Jacob conned Esau, (the elder of the two) out of his birth-right by offering him some food before it was served on the table (See Genesis 25:29-34) and had become, not surprisingly, a wanted man:

> "Esau held a grudge against Jacob because of the blessing his father had given him. He said to himself, 'The days of mourning for my father are near; then I will kill my brother Jacob.'" (Genesis 27:41)

Many years later, Jacob decided to try and make peace with his brother, Esau and sent a message via messengers suggesting that they meet up. Word came back that yes Esau would meet him but that he was coming with 400 men. Not surprisingly, Jacob was distressed to hear this and separated into two groups all those who were with him (family, servants, plus all his livestock). Jacob fell on the mercy of God for deliverance.

During that night, whilst on his own, Jacob wrestled with a man, who we are told was God:

> "So, Jacob called the place Peniel, saying, 'It is because I saw God face to face, and yet my life was spared.'" (Genesis 32:30)

At daybreak the man said, *"Let me go, for it is daybreak"*, but Jacob replied, *"I will not let you go until you bless me."* (v26)

Jacob understood the principle that I am getting at here. First, he prayed earnestly for deliverance from his brother and the armed men with him, then he would not let God go until he had blessed him. This is the earnest prayer and seizing hold of God that the phrase *grasping the horns of the altar* relates to. Yes, there is a desperation involved at times for God's mercy, but there is also a passion and earnestness about the prayer. It comes not from what we might say, but more from the fervour and intensity of prayer that comes from deep within us. This is commonly known as travailing prayer. The apostle Paul makes this observation:

> "We do not know what we ought to pray for, but the Spirit Himself intercedes for us through wordless groans. And He who searches our hearts knows the mind of the Spirit, because the Spirit intercedes for God's people in accordance with the will of God." (Romans 8:26-27)

We grasp the horns of the altar in the knowledge that God will not cast us out of His presence, but will turn His ear to our cries. I believe that if the church, as a whole, would get hold of this concept, then we will see and hear of building shaking prayer meetings. It will embolden us to come before God with seemingly outlandish prayers, but will receive the powerful answers from God which dramatically change those situations which once appeared tightly closed up.

There are those who are called to be intercessors, and are familiar with the above, yet I believe there is much more of a need for the church corporate to understand this concept and grasp hold of it. God moves mightily through the prayers of many. There is just something about a large gathering of people crying out to Him in earnest, intense prayer as we saw with the church in Acts 4.

The Altar of Sacrifice

The altar that was designated as a place of refuge as described in Exodus 21:12-14 was the large altar in the outer court used for the sacrifice of animals. For Christians in the New Covenant, there is no need for these because Jesus Himself, became the ultimate sacrifice. The writer to the Hebrews draws our attention to this in two places:

> "He sacrificed for our sins once for all when He offered Himself." (Hebrews 7:27)

and:

> "We have been made holy through the sacrifice of the body of Jesus Christ once for all." (Hebrews 10:10.)

For us now in the New Testament church, grasping hold of the horns of the altar is not made in desperation (although it may seem like it at times). It is with the confidence in knowing that Christ, being the ultimate sacrifice, triumphed gloriously over sin and death. Now, we too can know the victory for ourselves in the situations we find ourselves in:

> "Having cancelled the charge of our legal indebtedness, which stood against us and condemned us; He has taken it away, nailing it to the cross. And having disarmed the powers and authorities, He made a public spectacle of them, triumphing over them by the cross." (Colossians 2:14-15)

As we have seen with the church in Acts 4 and Moses' prayer in Exodus 33, God responds favourably when people come boldly and with confidence before Him in a way that we, in our righteousness, would deem not acceptable.

Chapter Eleven

The Design Brief

I wonder what the outcome would be if humans were given the responsibility for creating a design brief for their spiritual lives? At the very least, the brief should be inspired, inerrant and sufficient for each and every situation a person should ever come across. It should be all that that is needed to equip each of us, no matter what age, sex, colour, race or creed, for a life of faith and service to God. It should tell us all we ever need to know about God, His practices and behaviours and how we can know Him personally.

It is an incomprehensible thought. Thankfully we do not have to undertake this task as God has given us a design brief for our lives – yes, the Bible. In this sacred book, we find all we need to know about God, His great love for us and how we can have a deep and loving relationship with Him. Paul's second letter to Timothy articulates this aspect so well:

> "All scripture is God-breathed. It is useful for teaching, rebuking, correcting in righteousness so that the man or woman of God might be thoroughly equipped for every good work."
> (2 Timothy 3:16-17)

And there are so many other bible-verses we could use to show that these God-breathed scriptures are all we need for our Christian lives.

Included in the scriptures is certain guidance about the church, though unfortunately, there is no definitive check list of how to 'do' or 'be' church. We would perhaps say there is a lot that is missing from the bible that would enable us to get it exactly right. In Jesus' teachings and in the example of His relationship with God His Father, together with the book of Acts and the letters of Paul and others, we have more than just an outline of what Jesus expects from us as His church. He has made the Bible available to us so that we can examine and discover for ourselves what it has to say about different situations and how they apply to us.

There is no easy-to-follow list of how-to's and what-to-do's in the New Testament. Instead, we have to examine the whole of the NT to get a broad-brush concept of God's design-brief and what He had in mind. Coupled with this is the work of the Holy Spirit bringing to our attention Jesus's heart for His church – His Bride (as we saw in Ch. 1, *The Bride*)

What is Church?

As we have seen in previous chapters, in essence the word 'church' is a collective expression for a group of believers in Jesus, and the word church means an assembly of people. (This term was actually already in use in Jesus' time). So then, we see that what we mean when we think of church is that it's not a building, but people.

When Jesus told His disciples, "*I will build My church and the gates of Hades will not stand against it.*" (Matthew 16:18), I would imagine that Jesus had a pretty good idea of what He had in mind when He said this. As Jesus spoke of *building* His church, He wasn't meaning bricks and mortar. Strong's entry for the outline usage of this word says that build (Gr *oikodomeō*[12]) in this context means:

1. to found, establish
2. to promote growth in Christian wisdom, affection, grace, virtue, holiness, blessedness
3. to grow in wisdom and piety.

If we can disassociate ourselves from buildings and think in terms of people, we perhaps can begin to clue-in to the fact that Jesus in His teachings, whilst not specifically mentioning *church*, was actually preparing His disciples for their future mission once He had returned to heaven.

---

[12] Strong's Exhaustive Concordance G3618 - building

The Kingdom of God

Jesus spoke often about the 'kingdom of God' or the 'kingdom of heaven'. This phrase is more than just about the church. It is about attitudes, behaviours, responses toward and relations with people. So many of Jesus parables began with the statement, 'to what can I compare the kingdom of heaven…,' or 'the kingdom of God is like …' and then goes on to describe a nugget of wisdom about the kingdom.

If we think of the word *kingdom* it actually means 'kings' domain'. Strong's concordance says that the Greek word for 'kingdom', *basileia*[13] means royal power, kingship, dominion or rule and **'is not to be confused with an actual kingdom but rather is the right or authority to rule over a kingdom'** (my emphasis). Elsewhere, kingdom can also be defined as *the realm in which God's will is fulfilled*, which I find rather telling.

We know that Jesus gave the right and authority to the disciples (or apostles) during His last instructions to them (the Great Commission).

The right and authority to rule, coupled with God's redemptive will (that is He wants all people to be saved and come into the knowledge of his Son Jesus – 1 Timothy 2:4) has great implications for us as God's people. We now bear the right and authority as His representatives to carry out His will and commands, directives and guidelines as written in the scriptures.

The term *kingdom of heaven* is used exclusively by Matthew in his gospel whereas *kingdom of God* is used more widely in the New Testament and is a central theme across the gospels.

John the Baptist proclaimed that the *'kingdom of heaven is near'* (Matthew 3:2) thus pointing to a new order to come. When Jesus sent the twelve out on their first mission, He told them to *'proclaim this message: "The **kingdom of heaven** has come near"'*. (Matthew 10:7).

---

13 Strong's Exhaustive Concordance   G932 - kingdom

Luke records that they were to *'preach the kingdom of God'*. We should not get too hung up on the difference in these instructions as they have pretty much the same meaning.

In describing the kingdom, Jesus used everyday scenarios to help His listeners to understand what He was teaching them and while we may struggle to grasp some of them in this modern day and age, they are valuable in helping us to recognise the concepts of Jesus schooling.

Where Does the Church fit in?

In establishing that the church is an assembly of believers (or disciples) of Jesus, then it is this assembly who will carry the message of the kingdom of God to those around them. Therefore, should not much of what we do when we gather together as believers in our groupings be geared towards preparation and ongoing training in proclaiming the kingdom? The central message of Jesus was building the kingdom through proclaiming or preaching the kingdom.

Now we could say that when Jesus and the disciples preached about the kingdom of heaven, Jesus had not carried out His redeeming work on the Cross and subsequent Resurrection which would have changed much of the thrust and content of the disciple's mission and message. Yet Jesus, in teaching His disciples about the end of the age, said,

> "And this gospel of the kingdom will be preached in the whole world as a testimony to all nations". (Matthew 24:14)

So, we see here that Jesus called the message of the kingdom of God 'the gospel'. Luke also picks up on this:

> "The Law and the Prophets were proclaimed until John. Since that time, the good news (gospel) of the kingdom of God is being preached, and everyone is forcing their way into it." (Luke 16:16 - my insertion)

In the light of this, when we examine what actually happens in our church services, do we find the content of this principle of building and proclaiming the kingdom of God?

Thinking back over my 47+ years as a Christian I cannot remember a sermon on this aspect of the Kingdom of God. There may have been references to it but I cannot recall any extended series on this subject.

Now I know our very nature and conduct as Christians should be one of worship of and glory to, God. This is so eloquently affirmed in the Westminster Catechism (a summary of Christian doctrine in 107 questions and answers, completed in 1647 by the Westminster Assembly in London). In response to the very first question, *What is the chief end of man?* the answer is given, *Man's chief end is to glorify God, and to enjoy Him for ever.* Therefore, it could be said that worship is a mainstay of our services.

However, the ritual and tradition that make up the bulk of the services can be a distraction and hindrance to many in today's society. How often do we hear any reference to the kingdom of God as a principle that we should be promoting? The gospel that we are so familiar with is, I believe, far larger than we might have been taught or understand.

Gathering Together

So, what should we expect to find happening in a gathering of believers? There are a few indicators in the New Testament verses which give us a clue (Although many of these verses deal with the conduct of those gathering rather than giving a comprehensive list or set of instructions for any format of the meetings). This makes for a wide variation of what can be found occurring in churches, across the world.

There are many influences that will impact on our services, for example, demographics, culture and customs. Also, practical considerations such as where people meet and under what circumstances. These all play a part in determining the format of a church's activities when it meets.

We may be familiar with the verses in Acts that give us an insight to the activities of the early church:

> "They devoted themselves to the apostles' teaching and to fellowship, to the breaking of bread and to prayer. Everyone was filled with awe at the many wonders and signs performed by the apostles. All the believers were together and had everything in common. They sold property and possessions to give to anyone who had need. Every day they continued to meet together in the temple courts. They broke bread in their homes and ate together with glad and sincere hearts, praising God and enjoying the favour of all the people. And the Lord added to their number daily those who were being saved." Acts 2:42-47

We know that they met together in the temple courts, Solomon's Colonnade and in each other's homes, so there is evidence that the church was flexible about where it met. The meetings in one another's homes may have been because of opposition or practical reasons such as being unable to use or find a place suitable for them. I know from personal experience that meeting in a home can be a great setting as there is an informality which we do not find in a large or public building. However, recently I am hearing from God that it is more about His presence with believers when they gather, rather than it being about the place where worshippers meet.

Looking Through the Telescope

We know that a telescope is used to view things from a distance and that it has the effect of bringing an object closer and producing greater clarity. Conversely, if we look through the telescope from the wrong end it will make that object seem further away and make the focus less clear.

There is a well-known saying, 'looking through the telescope from the wrong end' which is an idiom meaning that a person is not considering the situation in the best way. I believe that in respect to the church, many are doing just this. Church has become an institution or organisation, a huge machine that has lost a lot of its original concept and purpose.

In considering the Kingdom of God and what part the church plays in this, we have to understand that the church is not *the* kingdom of God as some think. Rather, it is a *part*, which He uses to further His purpose. As we saw earlier, Jesus spoke much about this kingdom but mentioned the church infrequently. Quite surprisingly, church is only mentioned in two verses in Matthew's gospel and is not cited in any of the other gospels! Yet conversely, we find the phrase kingdom of God fifty-four times across all the gospels and kingdom of heaven occurs thirty-one times. Is this then telling us something?

As we saw earlier in this chapter the word kingdom means *the right or authority to rule over a kingdom and the realm in which God's will is fulfilled.* Therefore, when Jesus taught about the kingdom it was considerably more than just the church. Rather He was speaking about the activities He would expect to see His church engaged in.

Now you could say that the church is indeed engaged in the activities of the kingdom of God. However, we read of Jesus sending the twelve out on their first mission with the instructions:

> "As you go, proclaim this message: 'The kingdom of heaven has come near.' Heal those who are ill, raise the dead, cleanse those who have leprosy, drive out demons.'" (Matthew 10:7-8)

At the beginning of that chapter, before they were sent out, Jesus gave the disciples authority (Luke 9:1 has 'power and authority'). The kingdom of God is not a location, it is the authority of God within us.

So, when we speak of the church, we are speaking of those who have willingly submitted to God by asking Jesus to be a part of their lives, and have been given power through the Holy Spirit. They carry with them the authority of Jesus to carry out acts in His Name.

Signs and Wonders

In Mark's gospel, we read Jesus final instructions to His disciples before He ascends to heaven:

> "He said to them, 'Go into all the world and preach the gospel to all creation. Whoever believes and is baptised will be saved, but whoever does not believe will be condemned. And these signs

> will accompany those who believe: in my name they will drive out demons; they will speak in new tongues; they will pick up snakes with their hands; and when they drink deadly poison, it will not hurt them at all; they will place their hands on people who are ill, and they will get well."'
> (Mark 16:15-18)

Mark finishes the chapter by saying:

> "Then the disciples went out and preached everywhere, and the Lord worked with them and confirmed His word by the signs that accompanied it." (Mark 16:20)

Here then, I believe is what sets the early church apart from that which we find functioning today. Yes, there are churches in the UK who experience signs and wonders as part of their activities, yet sadly, they are in the minority. Why is this? We believe the same bible and the verses therein. We might sometimes preach on this aspect of service to God, but we do not generally see them in the everyday life of the church.

Why is this? Jesus said to His disciples (and to His church):

> "Very truly I tell you, whoever believes in me will do the works I have been doing, and they will do even greater things than these, because I am going to the Father." (John 14:12)

The intimation here is that those who believe In Jesus and follow Him as His disciples shall do these things. Yet, on the whole there is a scarcity of this taking place within today's church in the UK. Why is this?

First, I believe there has to be regular preaching and focus on signs and wonders. There are many who would say that we should be focusing on Jesus rather than on spurious manifestations. However, if Jesus deemed it necessary to tell His disciples to heal the sick, cast out demons etc, then who are we to dismiss these instructions or minimise this activity? Preaching will bring a focus onto a subject, raise faith and generate expectation in the hearts and minds of hearers.

Here then is a second reason: There is no expectation in the church for these to happen. It does appear to be a rule of the kingdom of God that expectancy and faith will lead to people seeing the supernatural happening in the church.

The culture of self-sufficiency and well-being in this modernistic 21st century, hampers any expectancy and, coupled with a lack of regular preaching and focus, lead to the dearth of signs and wonders being experienced in the church. Probably this has been the case throughout the ages, but it seems more concentrated and acute today.

I once read an account of some missionaries who worked in a region of Ethiopia in the 1930's. They were expelled from the country at the outbreak of the Second World War. Before they departed the missionaries left a basic translation in their language of John's gospel with the people.

At the end of the war, some of the missionaries managed to return to the region in Ethiopia. What they found was beyond their comprehension. Thousands of the indigenous people had become Christians and there were stories aplenty of miracles, signs and wonders. When the missionaries enquired what had been happening, they were told that the rudimentary versions of John's gospel had been read and preached among the people. When the missionaries discussed this amongst themselves there was a comment made, "We forgot to tell them that the signs and wonders of the gospel had now ceased."

"We forgot to tell them…" and it's a good thing that they did. Those unknowing people took God's word at face value, preached it, practiced it and saw it become reality in their lives. There is an account (again in John's gospel) where a royal official's son lay sick at Capernaum. When the official approaches Jesus and begs Him to "come down before my son dies", Jesus tells him, "You may go. Your son will live".

Now here's the crux of my argument here. After Jesus tells the official that his son will live, John records:

> "The man took Jesus at His word and departed." (John 4:50)

The man took Jesus at His word. That is what the missionaries found had been happening with the Ethiopians - they took Jesus at His word! Oh, what joy there would be in our churches if we were to see more of this taking place in our gathering together.

I once spent three weeks preaching on healing in the church I was leading. I knew there were many people in the congregation who had health issues. On the third week, at the end of my message, I called people forward who wanted Jesus to heal them. Only one person came forward. There was no expectancy in spite of the word of God being preached faithfully. This graphically highlights the uphill task preachers and leaders of churches have to bring their respective churches fully into line with God's Word in today's society.

This is not unusual in UK churches. We do not hear of regular healings or of signs and wonders. It seems that this aspect of our Christian lives has become neglected and relegated to the background, only receiving sporadic attention.

There is the whole discussion as to why this is and I do not want our attention to be deflected from the central point, but I find it very sad that a major command of Jesus in His last instructions to His disciples and consequently His church, has seemingly been as we say, kicked into the long grass.

But God's Word has this to say to us:

> "Consequently, faith comes from hearing the message, and the message is heard through the word about Christ."
> (Romans 10:17)

This verse comes after Paul has emphasised the need for the word of God to be preached to those who do not know Jesus, highlighting those who preach the word have been sent to do so. This is because they need the power of the Holy Spirit in their preaching to be effective.

Why did Jesus perform miracles, signs and wonders? It certainly wasn't for fame and renown as many times He hid Himself away after a miracle or sign or wonder had been wrought in a person's life. Equally, He often told the person receiving a healing not to tell anyone about this.

Jesus' miracles vindicated His claims about Himself and His teaching. They also showed His, and therefore God's, compassion and heart for people.

> "Do not believe me unless I do what my Father does. But if I do them, even though you do not believe me, believe the miracles, that you may know and understand that the Father is in me, and I in the Father." (John 10:37-38)

Here we see that Jesus encountered unbelief and that He is pointing those unbelievers towards the demonstration of the Spirit's power that was in Him.

The apostle Paul reminded the Corinthian church:

> "My message and my preaching were not with wise and persuasive words, but with a demonstration of the Spirit's power, so that your faith might not rest on human wisdom, but on God's power." (1 Corinthian 2:4-5)

If Jesus and Paul felt it was necessary to demonstrate God's power through the working of miracles to bring emphasis and reality to their message, shouldn't the church be earnestly seeking this in their ministry?

Regrettably, I believe the church of today has become settled and content with what they see happening (or not happening) in their midst. That is, one or two people being saved every so often, which seems to be enough to settle the conscience. There doesn't seem to be any realisation of the need for anything more. What they are experiencing is sufficient, thank you very much.

Chapter Twelve

The Church is a Building Site

If you have ever had any building work carried out at your home, either while still living in it or having vacated it until the work is completed, you will know that this is a messy and disrupting process. I have had experience of both scenarios, with my family being very glad when the work was over and the mess etc cleared away (and equilibrium restored.)

So, with this scenario in mind, how can I describe the church as being a building site?

One morning, as I was praying for the church my wife and I attend, I had a picture of additional supports being put in place beneath an upper floor. I had the impression that God was saying He was preparing to take the church to a new level, and that He was bringing in additional people to give support to the existing congregation who were already meeting together.

As I prayed about this picture, I found myself saying the words, *'the church is a building site'*. This could only have come from the Holy Spirit. I knew what God was saying through these words. He wasn't indicating that the church or ministry was a mess and needed repairs or refurbishment, but that He was referring to the continuous building work of Jesus' church.

Jesus told His disciples that *He would build His church* (Matthew 16:18) and it is the continued building of the church that I believe the phrase refers.

If we dissect the church and view the many components that we find across the vast breadth of the world-wide organisation (for that is what it is seen as), we see that Jesus is still building His church. New converts are being added by several thousand on a daily basis to the world-wide church. The ongoing mercy works shown to those in need continue to meet the new challenges that affect individuals and society in general. The ongoing Covid pandemic has thrown up immense challenges across the world and the church has been right there in the midst, being inventive and proactive in meeting the needs people have faced with this unprecedented experience and suffering.

Our local and national television news have highlighted some of the work churches have been involved in and it has been both heartening and heart-breaking to see what ministers, church leaders and members have faced and how they have been able to meet some of the challenges.

The gospel is still reaching unreached people groups. A recent article in Premier Christian News reported that YouVersion (who provide Bible reading resources) were joining forces with IllumiNations (an alliance of bible translation partners). This coming together supports a wide-ranging project to see the New Testament translated for 99.9% of the world population by 2033. Their raison d'etre is that the rapid development of technology and methodologies are accelerating translation work which now brings this goal within reach.[14]

Jesus is still building His church – it is a continuing work and thank God it is, because it means there is yet more room for people to be called into His kingdom and to be invited to His great banquet. Jesus continues to send His servants - you and I, out into the highways and byways to compel the lost to come in as we saw in chapter 3 - *A Great Harvest (2) - A Place for Revival.*

The apostle Paul writes:

> "I planted the seed, Apollos watered it, but God has been making it grow." (1 Corinthians 3:6)

God is still in the business of making the seeds of the gospel, that we have planted in people's lives, grow.

When the disciples asked Jesus about the signs of the end of the age, amongst other things He told them:

---
14 Premier Christian News report - Various sources

> "This gospel of the kingdom will be preached in the whole world as a testimony to all nations, and then the end will come." (Matthew 24:14)

As we have seen with the report on the acceleration of the work to make the New Testament available to 99.9% of world's populations, this prophecy is edging towards full realisation.

When we remind ourselves that the word 'church' used in the New Testament means an assembly of people, then to hear that Jesus is still gathering people to Himself should come as no surprise.

> "Because You were slain, and with Your blood You purchased for God, persons from every tribe and language and people and nation. You have made them to be a kingdom and priests to serve our God, and they will reign on the earth."
> (Revelation 5:9-10)

Jesus is still on His mission to gather people from across every part of the world. He is still building His church. The church is still a building site.

A building site will have a great variety of tradesmen and women bringing their many skills to it. Some will only be there for a specified period of time to carry out a particular task. Others will be on-site for the duration of the project. So then, we can envisage this aspect when we think of the church. There are those itinerant ministries that visit a church for a short period of time. For example, an evangelist or evangelistic team might be engaged for a church mission outreach and once that is completed, they move on to the next engagement or return to their own churches.

Within a congregation there will be those who preach the word, lead worship or who carry out other roles necessary to enable to church to exist and to grow. God has given spiritual gifts to enable believers to be effective in this work of building the church. (See Romans 12:4-8, 1 Corinthians 12:1-11 *et al.*) Whatever interpretation we use for this picture of the church as a building site, the overriding principle is that we understand Jesus has not finished building His church and will continue to develop it until He returns to earth at the end of the age to take His Bride to be with Him.

We are all Builders

The act of this building of Jesus' church has been cascaded down to individual fellowships and gatherings of individuals which the church comprises. It is the ordinary men and women who over the centuries Jesus has used and continues to use. Yes, there is a need for leaders and those who through learning, study and qualifications can interpret the bible and write commentaries etc, but the vast majority of the work is carried out by the foot soldiers.

We see this principle when we look at the book of Nehemiah. He was the man for the moment, used by God to rebuild the walls of Jerusalem. Nehemiah heard about the broken-down walls, burned doors of the city of Jerusalem, wept, and sought God about what was to be done.

Nehemiah was in a privileged position in the court of king Artaxerxes, and God used this to advantage. Nehemiah was granted leave of absence to go and survey the ruined walls of his home city and he put together a plan to rebuild the walls and gates etc. But it was the people of Jerusalem, the ordinary men and women in the street, who were used to do the building work. Each household rebuilt the section of wall immediately in front of their house. They weren't experienced builders, but with help from those who were, they managed to achieve the objective of repairing their allocation of the wall.

So, it is within our fellowships, churches and gatherings, that Jesus uses each one of us to build our part of His Church. Nehemiah experienced opposition from a pair of ne'er do wells, Sanballat and Tobiah, but after prayer the work carried on and was finished in record time – 52 days (Nehemiah 6:15).

The apostle Paul takes up a similar theme when he writes:

> "Brothers and sisters, think of what you were when you were called. Not many of you were wise by human standards; not

many were influential; not many were of noble birth. But God chose the foolish things of the world to shame the wise; God chose the weak things of the world to shame the strong. God chose the lowly things of this world and the despised things—and the things that are not—to nullify the things that are, so that no one may boast before Him. It is because of Him that you are in Christ Jesus, who has become for us wisdom from God - that is, our righteousness, holiness and redemption."
(1 Corinthians 1:26-30)

We only have to look at the eclectic mix of men who Jesus chose to spearhead the church to underpin the above model. The Sanhedrin called Peter and John *'unschooled, ordinary men'* (Acts 4:13). Among the twelve disciples were a tax collector, several fishermen, a zealot, two brothers who were hotheads (who at one time had wanted to call down fire from heaven in retribution for Samaritan opposition to Jesus) and others whom we know little about. We can guess they were representative of the general populace to whom they were minister to. Jesus knew what He was about when He gathered these guys together.

In addition, there were several women who followed Jesus. Mary Magdalene had been set free from seven demons, Joanna the wife of Chuza (a prominent royal official) and Suzanna, supported Jesus' ministry out of their own private means. All these people show us that Jesus' church is made up of individuals from all walks of life.

The church of today is not experiencing anything that God's people haven't faced before. The situations and involvements may have changed and they might look slightly different today but when stripped back we find that the church has already experienced similar before and has overcome them.

Chapter Thirteen

Looking Back to Move Forward

I was awake one morning at silly-o'clock – perhaps 4am. There was nothing wrong – just one of those things that happens now and then.

After a while, failing to return to my slumbers, I started thinking back over the last decade since my wife and I moved down to the South West of the UK, and pondered all that had happened over that time. We'd seen two of our sons get married, and bless us (to date) with five grandchildren. The hassle of trying to sell a house and buy another property, followed by the experience of renovating a bungalow and moving in; then building two extensions with my own hands.

I have now officially retired and joined the ranks of OAP's, enjoying the freedom to come and go, and the Jurassic coastline on which we now live. I thought back to the reason we originally moved down to this area – namely to be a part of a new church plant, having spent the many preceding months praying, and gaining God's perspective for us in this life-changing venture.

As part of the group of people who would form the nucleus of the new church, I was invited to become one of the leadership team – a new experience for me. I would later become an Elder of the church and eventually lead it for a while. I thought of the activities our new church embarked on – running an Alpha course, conferences, prayer weeks, prayer walks and a month of prayer and fasting.

We held a market stall every so often, giving out delicious hand-made cupcakes to passers-by in the town on a Saturday morning. People became Christians and we had baptismal services. We saw a new baby born to one of our couples, a 50th wedding celebration and had a wedding blessing for a newly married couple. Numbers grew and, on one Easter Sunday over 80 people attended the service. All-in-all it had all the hallmarks of a successful church plant.

As I reflected on these events, through my thoughts came this comment, "You did not ask Me". I turned this over in my mind for a few minutes and then it came again, "You did not ask Me".

I knew this second time that it was God speaking. I tried to comprehend what He was saying. I thought of the prayer times we had had, both as leaders and as a church.

This thought would not go away – somehow in all our busyness we had neglected to ask God about whatever matter we were involved in. Of course, we had prayed about them and sought God's wisdom and blessing, but somewhere along the line we hadn't actually asked God whether we should do a particular event.

How had we missed this? My thoughts went back to our initial Sunday meetings. The leadership team were experienced Christians of many years, but as I thought back, we assumed God was in what we were doing. We knew how to lead a meeting – we had seen it done often enough. Some worship, then a preach, and then tea and coffee and fellowship – we could do that no problem.

Then God directed me back to David who was anointed to be King of Israel. Although he was only a shepherd boy, he quickly gained a reputation for being a skilled leader and tactician. As David said to King Saul, when faced with the giant Goliath;

> "Your servant has been keeping his father's sheep. When a lion or a bear came and carried off a sheep from the flock, I went after it, struck it and rescued the sheep from its mouth. When it turned on me, I seized it by its hair, struck it and killed it. Your servant has killed both the lion and the bear".
> (1 Samuel 17:34-36)

This was David's training. Not so much in warfare but in bravery and fearlessness. As time went on, he became more and more skilled in the art of warfare, such was the degree that God was with him. And the point that God reminded me about, was that David enquired of the Lord.

His Intent

Even though David knew what he was doing and could have launched a successful attack on his enemies, yet he sought God's counsel. In 1 and 2 Samuel it is recorded that nine times David sought God's mind, before embarking on a mission.

There was a time when David did not seek God on a matter. 2 Samuel 6 tells of the story of when David tried to bring the Ark of the Covenant back to Jerusalem. He thought he knew how to do it, relying on his own knowledge and skill. He was by now the king of Israel and was expected to make decisions in front of his officials.

The Ark of the Covenant had been captured by the Philistines at Ebenezer (see 1 Samuel 4:1-11) but all the while they had it in their camp, things did not go well for them. After seven months they worked out what the problem was and sent the Ark back to the Israelites on a cart, pulled by a couple of oxen (1 Samuel 6).

It pitched up first at Beth-Shemesh and then was taken to Keriath-Jearim. After 20 years David determined to bring the Ark back to Jerusalem. So, he had a brand, spanking new cart made by the finest craftsmen in the land to transport it. A national holiday was called and a great day of celebration was planned. All was going well until one of the oxen stumbled and it looked as if the Ark was going to fall off the cart (2 Samuel 6).

A hapless guy called Uzzah stuck his hand out to steady the Ark. God immediately struck Uzzah down dead for touching the Ark. The party was over – no-one felt much like dancing anymore. David was distraught and angry with God for doing what He did to poor old Uzzah. After a period of reflection, word came through that the place where the Ark was stored – the house of Obed-Edom, had been mightily blessed by God. So, David made further enquiries and it was discovered how the Ark should have been transported – on poles carried on the shoulders of the Kohathites from the tribe of Levi (Numbers 4:15)

It is ironic that on those nine occasions mentioned earlier, 'David enquired of the Lord'. Time and again he went before the Lord before embarking on a mission. He could have set up ambushes against his enemies but before doing so he chose to go before God. On one occasion, God told David;

> (So David inquired of the Lord, and He answered) "Do not go straight up, but circle around behind them and attack them in front of the poplar trees. As soon as you hear the sound of marching in the tops of the poplar trees, move quickly, because that will mean the Lord has gone out in front of you to strike the Philistine army.'" (2 Samuel 5:23-24)

If only on that one occasion with the Ark David had asked God, it would have saved the life of Uzzah. Perhaps he had relied on self-sufficiency, we do not know. He might even have claimed ignorance about the method of moving the Ark. Maybe he rued his decision and shortcomings that time.

This, then, was what God was saying to me. We hadn't asked God about the basic matter of leading this new church. We had assumed and rested on our own knowledge and self-sufficiency. Yes, we knew how to run meetings etc but we hadn't asked God about them and so eventually things became unravelled.

At the time of writing, churches across the land are getting back into the swing of things again, emerging from the periods of lockdown caused by the Covid 19 pandemic. I am hearing people from a variety of national and international locations, saying that the church has to change; it cannot carry on as it has. It would appear that God is using this unique period of time to bring about change in His church across all denominations. This is radical, I admit. Many will protest that this is not God at all, and that it is those progressives who have been itching for an opening to introduce their agenda. After hearing these comments several times, I came to the conclusion that the Holy Spirit was speaking through people. And if this was so, then He was bringing the command from the very throne-room of God.

This sense that God wants to change the church is now being faced by the Anglican church in the UK. In June 2021 a briefing paper issued by the Church's Vision and Strategy group proposed the planting of 10,000 predominantly lay-led churches by 2030 if the church is to see any degree of growth. It cited stipendiary clergy, church buildings, and theological college training as "limiting factors" for growth.[15]

This proposal, not surprisingly, has touched off a firestorm of criticism and opposition and led to the formation of a Save our Parish group to defend the parochial system of the Church of England.

I sincerely believe that Jesus is speaking. While we have carried on pretty much the same for decades or even centuries, He is saying that we have to change. Sometimes it is helpful to look back (as I did) and see just where we have come from and where we missed the mark. In my case I did not feel that God was condemning me or any of the other leaders or what we had done:

> Therefore, there is now no condemnation for those who are in Christ Jesus. (Romans 8:1)
>
> For God did not send His Son into the world to condemn the world, but to save the world through Him. (John 3:17)

When God reminds us of something in our past it is not with condemnation, but because He wants to move us forward. In His own inimitable, loving way God showed me where we had fallen somewhat short and it did not take me long to understand what He was saying. However, as is so often the case, God gives us all another chance. He takes us around the block so-to-speak to let us get it right the next time.

Although I am no longer in any position of church leadership at the time of writing, God has given me a voice through the medium of recording podcasts and putting them on my website:
(www.discoverchristianity.co.uk/resources/podcasts).

Although not a large number listen to them it does enable me to share with others what I believe God is saying at this present time.

---

[15] Anglican Church's Vision and Strategy group - Various sources

If He is saying these things to me, then it is safe to say that He is speaking to others who may well have a greater influence and effectiveness.

The church my wife and I currently attend was established in 1653 and has been on its present site since 1699. It has a great inheritance through the dedicated labours of those who have gone before. We honour those ordinary men and women who faithfully followed the Lord and laboured to not only establish the church but to continue its witness and presence in the small coastal town in which it is situated.

However, although there have been many alterations to the building, including additional extensions, and changes to the format of the services and even language used, God is again speaking about change in this period in our rich history.

It would be all too easy for any church to form a committee or set up a working group to oversee any such changes or to decide which direction God might be leading the church. Yet, however this is progressed, we have to humble ourselves and ask God what is on His heart for this period of time. I would say that it has to include all parts of our functioning as churches. This will not be popular, as the Church of England is experiencing, since many of the church's gatherings have been shaped over the ages and it will be met probably with some resistance.

If we are to see the church emerging and progressing forward into all that God has in store for it, there have to be some very bold decisions taken (and humility displayed), recognising She belongs to Jesus. It was He who purchased men for God by His blood shed on the Cross. We are guardians and protectors of those whom He has placed under our care, and we have to change our emphasis and attitude towards this idea that we own the church. We may own the building in which we meet, but the people who are the church, have been bought at great cost by Jesus.

We as God's people, have the immense privilege of carrying forward Jesus' church in this 21st century and as we will see in Part II, God's intention is that through this diverse, eclectic church, His multi-faceted wisdom will be made known to the rulers and authorities in the heavenly realms. (Ephesians 3:10)

Part II

His Intent

"His intent was that now through the church the manifold wisdom of God might be made known to the rulers and authorities in the heavenly realms".
(Ephesians 3:10)

Introduction to Part II

Many bible scholars would say that there is great danger in isolating a particular verse on which to focus, as it detracts from the context. This can completely or largely miss the impact to which the other verses relate and the particular issue it wants to teach us. And yes, I would be thoroughly in agreement with this view.

However, there are times when we can concentrate on a single verse and find such riches in it that it doesn't necessarily detract from the context in which it sits. This then is the setting in which this book has been written. If we consider the preceding two verses of this chapter;

> "I became a servant of this gospel by the gift of God's grace, given me through the working of His power. Although I am less than the least of all the Lord's people, this grace was given me: to preach to the Gentiles the boundless riches of Christ, and to make plain to everyone the administration of this mystery, which for ages past was kept hidden in God, who created all things". (Ephesians 3:7-9)

Paul is giving the reason why he preaches the gospel to the Gentiles. Verse 11 explains the reasoning, namely that it was God's eternal purpose which was accomplished in Jesus.

This part is not intended to be a commentary but some considered thoughts that God has revealed and which the reader might have already considered themselves or have read in other publications.

Chapter Fourteen,

His Intent ...

As we commence our study into the foundational verse for this book, we look in detail at the wording used by Paul. At first reading the verse can be viewed as simply a statement, but as always with God's Word there is far, far more to be discovered.

From this verse, we see that the church is at the same time, historic, futuristic and in the here and now - in other words, past, present and future. I find it interesting that the NIV uses the word *was* when referring to God's intent. There is an inference here that, while this seems to have been God's original intention, there is now something else to replace His initial idea. However, this is not the case at all. There is no plan B when considering the church. In actual fact, the word *was* is peculiar to only three versions out of a total of forty-six that I have been able to view! It would therefore seem that the word *was* is only there to aid better reading.

I have had the wonderful privilege during my Christian life of sitting under some brilliant biblical scholars and teachers. They have shaped my love of scripture and taught me how to look beneath the surface of what we initially read, aided more than anything, by the Holy Spirit.

So, when reading Ephesians 3:10, my curiosity is aroused and this causes me to ask questions of the text.

First, when examining a single verse, we have to be cognisant of those verses either side – in our case v9 and v 11. In v9 (and other preceding verses) Paul is telling his readers how he has been humbled by the grace that God has been poured out into his life. Paul's commission to make known the mystery of the gospel to the Gentiles goes on in v 11 to tell that the wisdom that God reveals through the church is His eternal purpose, which has been accomplished through Jesus. So, we see that either side of our focus on v10 there is explanation to help us through.

Looking at the Greek rendering of this verse, we find that the words *His intent was* are not a part of it and although they form part of the focus of our interest, have only been put there (in the NIV) to aid better reading. However, although not in the Greek original, it does add emphasis and weight to our study.

When we read the words '*His intent*', we have to ask 'whose intent?' You might say, "Well it's obvious, is it not? It is God's intent." And you would be correct in saying that. But what does God's intent mean?

Intent can be defined as being directed with strained or eager attention, or having the mind, attention, or will concentrated on something or some end or purpose. It can also mean plan, resolved, determined, objective, target, purpose and so on.

God's plans being made known to humankind is nothing new. He showed Abraham His plan for His chosen people, the Israelites:

> I will make you into a great nation,
>   and I will bless you;
> I will make your name great,
>   and you will be a blessing.
> I will bless those who bless you,
>   and whoever curses you I will curse;
> and all peoples on earth
>   will be blessed through you. (Genesis 12:2-3)

He showed Moses the plans for the Tabernacle (Exodus 26:30) and of course there is the well-known verse in Jeremiah about God's plans for us:

> For I know the plans I have for you," declares the LORD, "plans to prosper you and not to harm you, plans to give you hope and a future. (Jeremiah 29:11)

God plans ahead. He is streets ahead of anything humans can envisage or bring into reality. He planned the earth and everything that would be upon it. Creationist scientists will reel off a whole host of facts about the fine-tuning and balance that the earth is held in, enabling it to sustain life and to remain in existence. Facts such as the tilt of the earth at twenty-three and a half degrees which governs the seasons and the temperatures we experience. In addition, we are approximately ninety-three million miles from the sun – a distance that just so happens to ensure that we as humans can survive to a large degree most of the temperature range we encounter here on the earth.

And so, we could go on. The creation of the earth points, despite what critics and others say, to an intelligent, planning and designing God.

But there is one plan of God that surpasses all others and that is His plan for the human race. God wanted to show and demonstrate His great love to us. First, He created us for His pleasure (Revelation 4:11 - KJV). Can you imagine this? That the God who created the universe, set stars into place, put the planets in their positions and orbits and decided to make human beings - just because He can. And He wanted to demonstrate His great love towards those He created.

God created mankind to show His great glory and demonstrate His love for us:

> The heavens declare the glory of God; the skies proclaim the work of His hands. (Psalm 19:1)
>
> Lord, our Lord, how majestic is Your name in all the earth! You have set Your glory in the heavens... When I consider Your heavens, the work of Your fingers, the moon and the stars, which You have set in place, what is mankind that You are mindful of them, human beings that You care for them?"
> (Psalm 8:1, 3-4)
>
> For in Him all things were created: things in heaven and on earth, visible and invisible, whether thrones or powers or rulers or authorities; all things have been created through Him and for Him." (Colossians 1:16)

1 John 4:8 tells us that *God is love*. His very essence is love. Strong's concordance entry for this word love – Greek *agape,* means affection,

good will, love, benevolence. It is at the very root of what God does and why He does it.

We as a human race did not just appear on earth, but we were planned with meticulous precision. Genesis 3 tells us that God formed us with His own hands and then breathed His breath into our nostrils. If you've ever held a new-born baby – just a few minutes old in your hands you will appreciate something of this loving, tender act of God.

This plan of God was instigated with a purpose – an intent. Yet at first it appeared that God's plan had been derailed. The perfect and passionate relationship between God and the first humans on earth – Adam and Eve became separated through their sin. They disobeyed God's command to not touch or eat the fruit of one particular tree, but they were deceived by satan, and so became separated from God, which had an everlasting implication for the rest of humanity. Through this one act of disobedience, we all have been separated from God and subsequently, from a loving relationship with Him.

However, all is not lost. In His foreknowledge, God had known this separation would come about and provided a plan of salvation, whereby we would once again be reunited with Him. His dearly loved Son, Jesus would stand in place of us before God and become sin for us, would take the punishment that sin deserves and so reconcile us to God.

In doing this Jesus would birth the church, a chosen people who would represent Him on earth.

It is this church that we have looked at over the preceding chapters and which forms the next in our study.

Chapter Fifteen

Through the Church

When Jesus met with His disciples at what we know as the Last Supper, He introduced a new covenant to them. The existing covenant under Mosaic law required daily sacrifices of animals as a reminder of people's sin, but the writer to the Hebrews tells us:

> "For it is not possible that the blood of bulls and of goats should take away sins". (Hebrews 10:4)

and

> "… the ministry Jesus has received is as superior to theirs (the priests who administered the Old Covenantal sacrifices) as the covenant of which He is mediator is superior to the old one, since the new covenant is established on better promises. For, if that first covenant had been faultless, then should no place have been sought for the second".
> (Hebrews 8:6-7 - my insertion)

By ushering in this new covenant – the generally accepted idea of binding or establishing a bond between two parties, Jesus was saying that in effect, the Old Covenant had served its purpose. Now Jesus was bringing in a new era in the purposes and plan of God.

Jesus was now to be the ultimate sacrifice. This meant no other means would be needed or indeed would be able to meet the requirements of God's perfect law.

As Jesus introduced this concept to His disciples, He did so by telling them that the bread that He broke and which they ate and the wine they drank, were to be symbols of His body and His blood which He was soon to shed, not only for them, but for the whole world.

It is important for us to understand this New Covenant established through the death and resurrection of Jesus form the very foundation of the church. Jesus was now to be revealed as the reconciler between the human race and God. He would be the One who bring together people from every language, race and tongue. They would enjoy the kind of relationship with Him that had been longed for by those who had previously sought earnestly after Him.

These people would become the church – the assembly of God's people that Peter speaks of in his 1st letter to the church – God's elect:

> "But you are a chosen people, a royal priesthood, a holy nation, God's special possession, that you may declare the praises of Him who called you out of darkness into His wonderful light. Once you were not a people, but now you are the people of God; once you had not received mercy, but now you have received mercy." (1 Peter 2:9-10)

Jesus' work on the Cross means that we are now able to enjoy relationship with Him and God the Father in a way only imagined by those of the Old Testament times. It is because of this that Paul was inspired to write the verse we are considering.

Now Through the Church ...

I want to focus on the word *'now'* for a while. It speaks of an immediacy, that things are going to be different. Once what existed, is no longer the case. Now there is a new focus on God and His Son Jesus. It tells the reader that until this particular time in history, the mystery of salvation has not been disclosed to the world and the powers and authorities in the heavenly realms. This mystery is the coming together of Gentiles and Jews, under one head – Jesus, and will be known as the church – the body of Christ. The early church must have struggled no end to comprehend this coming together under one roof, so to speak. For centuries there had been separation between the two, but now the Holy Spirit had been poured out on both Jew and Gentile and they could worship together.

This coming together in the Name of Jesus was to be a powerful demonstration of the reconciling work of Jesus on the Cross. The apostles were given wisdom to understand what God was doing – first demonstrated when Peter addressed the crowds at Pentecost;

> "In the last days, God says,
>   I will pour out my Spirit on all people.
> Your sons and daughters will prophesy,
>   your young men will see visions,
>   your old men will dream dreams.
> [18] Even on my servants, both men and women,
>   I will pour out my Spirit in those days,
>   and they will prophesy". (Acts 2:17-18)

Peter and others were to realise this further when they went to Cornelius' house:

> "The circumcised believers who had come with Peter were astonished that the gift of the Holy Spirit had been poured out even on Gentiles". (Acts 10:45)

This coming together from both sides of the divide as it were, would be the strength and weight that would propel the new church into the forefront of God's mission on the earth. This strength comes from our togetherness in Christ. It joins people from disparate backgrounds, experiences and environments that in the natural realm would be difficult or nigh impossible to achieve. But they do work alongside each other, not only in a surface agreement but with deep and meaningful expressions of love, closeness and friendship.

We see the beginnings of this development in a description of the early church in a well-known passage Acts:

> "They devoted themselves to the apostles' teaching and to fellowship, to the breaking of bread and to prayer. Everyone was filled with awe at the many wonders and signs performed by the apostles. All the believers were together and had everything in common. They sold property and possessions to give to anyone who had need. Every day they continued to meet together in the temple courts. They broke bread in their homes and ate together with glad and sincere hearts, praising God and enjoying the favour of all the people. And the Lord added to their number daily those who were being saved".
> (Acts 2:42-47)

Paul had written earlier in this letter about the divisions that once existed:

> "Remember that at that time you were separate from Christ, excluded from citizenship in Israel and foreigners to the covenants of the promise, without hope and without God in the world". (Ephesians 2:12)

But he then goes on to show how Jesus has joined the two sides together:

> "But now in Christ Jesus you who once were far away have been brought near by the blood of Christ. For He himself is our peace, who has made the two groups one and has destroyed the barrier, the dividing wall of hostility, by setting aside in His flesh the law with its commands and regulations. His purpose was to create in Himself one new humanity out of the two, thus making peace, and in one body to reconcile both of them to God through the cross, by which He put to death their hostility". (Ephesians 2:13-16)

Note Paul says (Jesus) *has made the two groups one and has destroyed the barrier, the dividing wall of hostility, by setting aside in His flesh the law with its commands and regulations*. The old divisions have been dissolved and now there is a new order. The Holy Spirit has encompassed both Jew and Gentile and shown them that they could work together and actually enjoy one another's company. They now have a new focus and freedom to worship God in a way that they had never experienced before. No longer are there constrictions and restraints by man's directions and adherence to a strict set of rules and directives, but now they are free to worship God from their experience with the Holy Spirit.

The church, when she is firing on all cylinders, is indeed a force to be reckoned with. We see this in the early chapters of Acts when even in the face of hostility and persecution, and being scattered, the Gospel was spreading significantly. There was exceptional growth with new people being added daily. People were being healed from all manner of sicknesses and diseases and were set free from demonic possession and influence. Although the fear of God permeated their actions and gatherings, nevertheless, people were still added to their number (Acts 5:12-16)

It is this church that God uses to demonstrate His wisdom (as we shall see in the next chapter). The church has much that needs attention in order to bring it back into line with God's original intent. However, the mystery is, that although the church leaves much to be desired in today's world, this is still the means through which God demonstrates His sovereign purpose.

The church which we spent the first part of this book examining, is the means through which God makes Himself known to the world around us. There is still a very real place for her in today's society. God has not abandoned the church – indeed as we saw in the first chapter *The Bride* there will be a glorious celebration at the consummation of the Bride and the Bridegroom at the wedding of the Lamb of God. We must not lose sight of this fact, even though we might feel that God would be better served if the church was scrapped and He started afresh with a new plan.

Yes, the church is in need of reform and renewal, but rather than disbanding and winding it up, God in His infinite wisdom chooses to work within and through her.

The words that began this chapter, *Now through the church,* are still as relevant for today as they were when Paul wrote them. This assembly of people which we looked at in Chapter 5 – *What is the Church?* is the most astounding and wonderful aspect of this verse. This eclectic mix of people will be the ones that God uses to display and reveal His manifest, multi-faceted wisdom to the powers and authorities in the heavenly realms.

This means you and I! Yes, it is amazing that God should choose to use people such as you and I for this task. Through our walk with His Son, Jesus we display the wisdom of God the Father. The apostle Paul makes this seem even more miraculous when he writes:

> "Brothers and sisters, think of what you were when you were called. Not many of you were wise by human standards; not many were influential; not many were of noble birth. But God chose the foolish things of the world to shame the wise; God chose the weak things of the world to shame the strong. God chose the lowly things of this world and the despised things - and the things that are not—to nullify the things that are, so that no one may boast before Him. It is because of Him that you are in Christ Jesus, who has become for us wisdom from God - that is, our righteousness, holiness and redemption".
> (1 Corinthians 1:26-30)

In other words, ordinary men and women such as you and I. People who would not consider themselves any great shakes, just going about their ordinary day-to-day business. Not making any great impact on life or the church, yet collectively demonstrating and exhibiting the wisdom of God.

Recently, God has shown me that just being a part of a church and in the congregation on a Sunday or other occasion, speaks massively of the glory and triumph of Jesus on the Cross.

> "And having disarmed the powers and authorities, He made a public spectacle of them, triumphing over them by the Cross".
> (Colossians 2:15)

Many Christians disqualify or belittle themselves by saying "I can't play an instrument, or sing very well, or preach, so I haven't got anything to offer the church". But every time we, as believers, gather together we declare yet again the victory of Christ over the evil one. There is a massive statement in the heavenly realms by us just being together in a church. It yet again declares "God is alive and Jesus' victory still stands". We cannot underestimate the power that is displayed to the powers and authorities in the heavenly realms by a group of redeemed sinners worshipping the risen Saviour!

In the next chapter we will explore what the wisdom of God is.

Chapter Sixteen

The Manifold Wisdom of God

As we saw at the end of the previous chapter, Paul writes about how God uses ordinary men and women going about their everyday lives to display the wisdom of God.

We saw that this wisdom from God is through Jesus:

> "Christ Jesus, who has become for us wisdom from God - that is, our righteousness, holiness and redemption".
> (1 Corinthians 1:30)

and so, now we explore and develop our understanding of God's wisdom. It is notable that Paul uses the word manifold to describe this wisdom of God. There are many diverse synonyms that are used in different versions – multi-faceted, rich variety, full-diverse, wisdom in all its different forms, innumerable aspects, and there are many other words that could be used to describe this wisdom of God.

However, whichever term is used for this wisdom, it must be looked at through the lens of the church, as this is what Paul had in mind when he wrote the letter to the Ephesians.

It is through the church, this assembly of God's people, that His diverse wisdom is revealed. It is worth mentioning that the way this verse is written in the Greek, the wisdom of God comes at the end, viz:

> "Now to the rulers and authorities in the heavenly realms through the church; the manifold wisdom of God".

Paul said earlier that his mission was to make plain to everyone the administration of the mystery of Christ, which for ages was kept hidden (Ephesians 3:9). Then he launches into v10 by declaring that

God's intent is that *now* through the church this wisdom of God is being made known.

God's wisdom has a great many faces to it. We can look at the wisdom books – Job, Psalms, Proverbs, Ecclesiastes, Song of Songs. Then there are the great many other verses describing or referring to God's wisdom. People like Solomon displayed God's wisdom. Paul writes in his letter to the Romans:

> "Oh, the depth of the riches of the wisdom and knowledge of God!
> How unsearchable His judgments,
>   and His paths beyond tracing out!
> 'Who has known the mind of the Lord?
>   Or who has been His counsellor?'
> 'Who has ever given to God,
>   that God should repay them?'
> For from Him and through Him and for Him are all
> things.
> To Him be the glory forever! Amen".
> (Romans 11:33-36)

Here Paul is taken up with the glory of this wisdom (and knowledge of God) such that he breaks off from writing his letter and bursts into this doxology. One can easily get caught up with this when reading this part of Romans, as he reveals something of God's plans for the church and how it fits into His sovereign plan for Israel. Paul sees in the Spirit, God's wisdom of this mystery which is revealed to us through his writing.

Returning to the wisdom of God that Paul refers to in Ephesians 3:10, it seems he is speaking about both the mystery of Christ and the mystery of the church as it is revealed to the powers and authorities in the heavenly realms. I am sure there have been and still are, many Christians who scratch their heads and wonder why God instituted the church. As we look back, we can see almost a trail of wreckage in the activities of the church that have done nothing to further the work of God and Jesus in particular.

However, God in His wisdom, will bring all things together at the end of the age. We may look aghast at the church and wonder how God will ever be able to bring all the diverse sections together in a way that will bring glory to Him. I freely admit it seems an impossibility, but (and it is a big but) God in His infinite wisdom will do this so that it will display His own wisdom.

John Stott writes in his commentary on the book of Ephesians:

> In this new phenomenon, this new multi-racial humanity, the wisdom of God was being displayed. Indeed, the coming into existence of the church, as a community of saved and reconciled people, is at one and the same time a public demonstration of God's power, grace and wisdom: first of God's mighty resurrection power, next of His immeasurable grace and kindness and now thirdly of His manifold wisdom[16]

The word manifold also has Old Testament connections: The Greek word *poikilos* in the Septuagint (the Old Testament translated into Greek) is used when describing Joseph's coat of many colours (Genesis 37:3, 23, 32).

This manifold wisdom of God is shown through the church in a variety of colours and hues. It comes through the great diversity of people that we find in God's church across the globe. As we are told in the book of Revelation:

> "After this I looked, and there before me was a great multitude that no one could count, from every nation, tribe, people and language, standing before the throne and before the Lamb. They were wearing white robes and were holding palm branches in their hands". (Revelation 7:9)

God's wisdom is revealed through the church so that we are in fact a reflection of it.

There is a saying that comes from a scene in the William Shakespeare comedy *As You Like It* when the melancholy Jaques utters the immortal

---

16 The Message of Ephesians John Stott

words *"The world is the stage"*. Several Bible commentors pick up on this when referring to the church's role in society, and they observe that the actors are the church and that the play has been written and is directed by God Himself. Scene by scene the play is revealed as it is acted out by the church.

The audience is the rulers and authorities in the heavenly realms, whom we shall deal with in greater detail in the next chapter.

God's wisdom can never be totally understood or said to be fully revealed to mankind. As Paul wrote in Romans 11 (as mentioned earlier) *"Oh the depth of the riches of the wisdom and knowledge of God! How unsearchable His judgments, and His paths beyond tracing out! Who has known the mind of the Lord?"* (vs 33-34a)

There is just no way we will ever know completely about the wisdom of God. How many times have we viewed a situation and afterwards been able to see the wisdom of God that has enabled that circumstance to be resolved?

Paul does have some insight into this aspect of God's wisdom when he writes in his first letter to the Corinthian church:

> We do, however, speak a message of wisdom among the mature, but not the wisdom of this age or of the rulers of this age, who are coming to nothing. No, we declare God's wisdom, a mystery that has been hidden and that God destined for our glory before time began. (1 Corinthians 2:6-7)

The wisdom from God, has to be *revealed* to us. It is not something that comes naturally to us – even once we become Christians. Now it may seem that this makes for a capricious God – someone who plays hide and seek with us - but even in this it is His wisdom that decides what to reveal to us and when. God does all this for our good and for His glory. This is not to say He is self-seeking but He knows what is best for us and we in turn give Him glory for those things His wisdom reveals to us. It leaves us in awe and wonder of Him and His ways.

Paul again makes reference to the mystery of God, which we saw earlier in Ephesians 3:9. The whole plan of God, the whole play is a mystery that keeps us on the edge of our seats as it is revealed piece by piece, scene by scene.

Just like a wise parent, God knows just what we can cope with, and as students of our life in Christ, His wisdom and ways are disclosed in a way that we can deal with. I am sure that, like me you have been glad that God has not always chosen to unveil everything at once or you would have felt swamped. In these situations, we recognise this as being the wisdom of gradually unfolding.

That God should choose to unfold His multi-faceted wisdom though the church is indeed a wonder in itself. We can look at her and both marvel and puzzle at the wisdom of His working through this dysfunctional, eclectic mix of people to achieve His sovereign purpose.

Yet we can have confidence that God knows what He is doing. He has a sovereign plan in which He involves all of us to achieve it.

Isaiah says:

> "For my thoughts are not your thoughts,
>   neither are your ways my ways,"
> declares the LORD.
> "As the heavens are higher than the earth,
>   so are my ways higher than your ways
>   and my thoughts than your thoughts.
> As the rain and the snow
>   come down from heaven,
> and do not return to it
>   without watering the earth
> and making it bud and flourish,
>   so that it yields seed for the sower and bread for the eater,
> so is my word that goes out from my mouth:
>   It will not return to me empty,
> but will accomplish what I desire"
> (Isaiah 55:8-11)

Although not directed towards the church, this passage serves to remind us of the sovereignty of God and that He is over and above anything that we can imagine or even think.

The amazing factor to remember is that it is God's desire that we, the church, are involved in the revealing of His wisdom to the powers and authorities in the heavenly realms. As we ponder on this wonderful and glorious truth, we can say with confidence that this is our heavenly Father, who wants us to be involved. No one is excluded. It is only the enemy who sows seeds of doubt that result in our self-disqualification from this.

God, in His foreknowledge has predestined us, hand-picked us to be a part of His plan being unveiled before men and angels. He did this before the foundations of the earth were laid (Ephesians 1:4). He did this even knowing what we would be like. He knew everything about us – all our foibles, all our shortcomings, all our abilities, everything. And yet He still chose us to be a part of Jesus' glorious church.

God is working in and through the church, to display and declare His amazing, confounding, deep and rich wisdom to the world and the heavens. Remember that He knows what He is doing and will continue to work out His sovereign plan using ordinary men and women such as you and I.

The church's history reveals Christians who not only made an impact on the society in which they circulated, but also announced to the heavenly beings her prominence and God's great wisdom. Some are well known, but others, known only to God, have served quietly and faithfully in the background.

Chapter Seventeen

Rulers and Authorities

Over the course of this book, we have explored the church, its foundation and hope that is to come. We have looked at the subject text as it relates to the church. We now come towards the climax of our studies, the culmination of the exploration of this single verse.

In our study we have only really skimmed the surface of the meaning and application of this verse, no one person being able to plumb the depths of the richness of its application. The fullness will only be realised and made known at the completion of God's eternal and sovereign plan.

Probably without fully knowing or understanding, Paul has opened up to us a wonderful insight to the power of the church and that her very existence shouts, even roars, across the heavens and declares the glory and wisdom of God. Psalm 19:1a tells us, *The heavens declare the glory of God,* and in this one short statement, there carries the immense weight and depth of meaning, which we as finite beings only get a glimpse of in its implications. In the same way the church announces to the heavenly powers and authorities the wisdom and majesty of God.

The church preaches to the heavens the victory of Christ through its very existence. Whilst oppressors have tried many and varied ways to obliterate the church and rid the earth of it, yet, like a ball submerged in water and then released, it bounces back to the surface. Everything the devil and his cohorts have thrown at the church has resulted in failure and humiliation for them.

The church, by its very existence on the earth, proclaims and shouts aloud across the heavenlies the wisdom of God in persisting with her. As we saw in Chapter 1, *The Bride,* the church has been promised to His Son, Jesus as His bride and God will not break His promise.

Rulers and Authorities

The church carries, in God's kingdom, a declaration of who she is and proclaims the victory of Jesus on the Cross.

> And having disarmed the powers and authorities, He (Jesus) made a public spectacle of them, triumphing over them by the cross. (Colossians 2:15 - my insertion)

I absolutely love this verse as it speaks of Jesus' total and utter dominance and supremacy over all the powers and authorities that are at work in this world and the heavenlies.

Several commentators see this announcing of God's wisdom as being directed only to the angels who surround God's throne, but Paul doesn't give any hint that this is all he is meaning in Ephesians 3:10.

The writer to the Hebrews tells us that angels are ministering spirits to those who will inherit salvation:

> Are not all angels ministering spirits sent to serve those who will inherit salvation? (Hebrews 1:14)

There is a whole branch of theology called *Angelology* which examines what the Bible teaches about the entire subject of angels. Suffice to say for our purposes here, that the powers and authorities that Paul includes in Ephesians 3:10 are more than just angels per se.

So, who are the rulers and authorities that Paul refers to? I believe he is speaking of the whole cosmos that is influenced or infiltrated by these powers and authorities. We can get some indication by viewing the last chapter of Ephesians:

> Put on the full armour of God, so that you can take your stand against the devil's schemes. For our struggle is not against flesh and blood, but against the rulers, against the authorities, against the powers of this dark world and against the spiritual forces of evil in the heavenly realms. (Ephesians 6:11-12)

Note here that Paul speaks of *this dark world*, thus indicating that these rulers, authorities and powers are not a part of heaven in which Christ dwells. Here, Paul gives us an insight into who it is we are up against as God's people and therefore the church. First, he speaks of the devil's schemes. 1 John 5:19 tells us that *the whole world is under the control of the evil one* and 2 Corinthians 4:4 reveals that *the god of this age has blinded the minds of the unbelievers.* Therefore, there is arrayed against the people of God the forces of evil and the devil's armies.

It is interesting that when Jesus was in the wilderness being tempted by the devil, when speaking of all the kingdoms of the world He says:

> I will give you all their authority and splendour, for it has been given to me, and I can give it to anyone I want to. (Luke 4:6)

Note here that the devil says his authority has been given to him. Where then did he get it from? We know from Revelation 12:7-9 that there was a war in heaven and the devil was defeated and was cast out of heaven. He lost any authority and position he held then, so where did he pick it up again, or was it relinquished to him by someone?

We read in Genesis 3 how the serpent – who, in reality was satan, tempted Eve, who in turn led her husband, Adam, into sin. Here then, was the transfer or relinquishing of Adam's authority into the hands of satan. In effect, handing over the keys of that authority to the devil.

It wasn't until Jesus' death on the Cross that He completely defeated death and Hades and took back the keys of authority:

> I am the Living One; I was dead, and now look, I am alive for ever and ever! And I hold the keys of death and Hades. (Revelation: 1:18)

In doing so, Jesus has disarmed these powers and now, through the church – including you and me, the wisdom of God is being made known. As we saw in the last chapter, it is the continuation of the church, in spite of what the devil has thrown at her down through the ages, that declares the wisdom and majesty of God.

The brilliant part of all this is that we as God's people, although once a part of this kingdom of darkness, are no longer so:

> For He has rescued us from the dominion of darkness and brought us into the kingdom of the Son He loves, in whom we have redemption, the forgiveness of sins. (Colossians 1:13-14)

Every time a person becomes a Christian, they step into God's kingdom, and the wisdom of God is declared once again to the powers of darkness:

> I tell you that in the same way there will be more rejoicing in heaven over one sinner who repents than over ninety-nine righteous persons who do not need to repent. (Luke 15:7)

> In the same way, I tell you, there is rejoicing in the presence of the angels of God over one sinner who repents. (Luke 15:10)

When we think of the thousands each day who give their lives to Jesus, there is a lot of rejoicing in heaven – a continuous party taking place over repentant sinners. There is literally a roar going up in heaven as each person steps across that line into the kingdom of heaven. This raucous celebration reaches the ears of those powers and authorities who stand opposed to Jesus and must be a continuous source of irritation – like a stone in a shoe or a thorn in the flesh to them.

The new believers shout out Christ's Lordship over the rulers and authorities and across the heavens. When Jesus rose from the dead, He declared in this one action the power and supremacy of God:

> His incomparably great power for us who believe. That power is the same as the mighty strength He exerted when He raised Christ from the dead and seated Him at His right hand in the heavenly realms, far above all rule and authority, power and dominion, and every name that is invoked, not only in the present age but also in the one to come. (Ephesians 1:19-21)

That power is made known through us the church. Is it any wonder then that the church makes known to the powers and authorities the wisdom of God? When the church is functioning as Jesus designed it, then we blast it out across the heavens that Jesus is Lord and He is seated at the right hand of God. I struggle to put into words what I am discerning in my spirit about this. It speaks of triumph and victory that we the church can claim and plug into. It makes me wonder why the devil, knowing he has been defeated and remains so, continues to try and gain the upper hand over the church.

Having said all this, we must not diminish, under-estimate or overlook the effect these powers and authorities have (or try to have) on us here on earth – especially those who are outside of Christ.

> Be alert and of sober mind. Your enemy the devil prowls around like a roaring lion looking for someone to devour.
> (1 Peter 5:8)

As we saw earlier, Paul alerts the church to this strategy when he writes:

> For our struggle is not against flesh and blood, but against the rulers, against the authorities, against the powers of this dark world and against the spiritual forces of evil in the heavenly realms (Ephesians 6:12)

Therefore, we have a very real battle on our hands. These powers and authorities are literally hell-bent on destroying the church – you and me, but Jesus gives us His promise that those gates of hell will not overcome us (Matthew 16:18). One wonders why these powers and authorities continue their onslaught against us, but for them the issue is 1) preventing people becoming a Christian in the first place and 2) trying to waylay or generally mess up our walk with Jesus.

As long as there is a church here on earth, we testify by the very existence of it, the wisdom of God in establishing and persisting with it.

Although perhaps here on earth, the church in some parts of the world, may seem somewhat disorganised or dying, yet in the heavenlies and here on earth her very existence continues to declare the majesty and splendour of God. This is being worked out in the lives of redeemed human beings through the death and resurrection of Christ.

As I mentioned at the close of the previous chapter, there has been a steady procession of those faithful servants of God who have quietly gone about their service to Him. Equally, there have been many whom

God has chosen to raise up and place centre stage in society and who have done great exploits for Him. One can think of the Wesley brothers, George Whitefield, Smith Wigglesworth, Kathryn Kuhlman, Aimee Semple McPherson, Charles H Spurgeon, Dr Martyn Lloyd-Jones and many, many others each of whom, in their own way, have made a great impact in their day.

In various parts of the globe news and reports filter through of churches and individuals who are having a major impact on the kingdom of darkness, seeing people healed, set free from demonic affliction and even people being raised from the dead! These Christians are fighting against the powers and authorities that Paul speaks of in Ephesians 6:12 – 18 and seeing God back their message up with signs and wonders following. It is people like these who are blasting out across the heavenlies the manifold wisdom of God.

There is a glorious future for the Church both here on the earth and in the marriage to the Lamb of God. There is much that needs addressing within the church but we must not let this colour our image of how God sees her. He sees great potential still as she moves exorably forward in the purposes of God and according to His great plan of redemption for humankind.

Chapter Eighteen

Wrapping Things Up!

We have taken a look at the church, which has been by-no-means exhaustive, seeing that she is betrothed to her bridegroom, Jesus, and is working towards the final consummation when they are joined together as God the Father intended. We have seen the glorious plans that He has for the church in making His wisdom known to those spiritual authorities that reign (for a period of time) in the heavenlies.

In the introduction to Part II, I referred to the dangers of focussing on just one verse in a chapter as it can isolate it from the context in which it was written. As we come to the end of this book and reflect on our journey, I want to expand Ephesians 3:11-12 to, as-it-were, tie up the remaining loose ends to our studies:

> …according to His eternal purpose that He accomplished in Christ Jesus our Lord. In Him and through faith in Him we may approach God with freedom and confidence.
> (Ephesians 3:11-12)

We can clearly see that verse 11 is a direct continuation of verse 10. Verse 10 has a comma at its end rather than a full stop, so the two go hand-in-hand. Paul indicates in verse 11 that this wisdom of God is an outcome of His eternal purpose – that the church, her influence and very existence is very much a part of God's eternal purpose – which He ordained and decreed before the foundations of the earth, all of which He accomplished through His Son, Jesus.

Note, Paul declares that this whole aspect of the church making known the manifest wisdom of God, has already been achieved through Christ. The words *He accomplished* has the inference, confirmation and assertion that it has already been finalised and secured - not might be, not may be, but *has* already been done. Paul also emphasises this in his letter to the Colossians:

> And having disarmed the powers and authorities, He made a public spectacle of them, triumphing over them by the Cross. (Colossians 2:15)

The work that Jesus completed on the Cross accomplished all that Paul speaks of in Ephesians 3:10-12 and more. In addition, we now have freedom of access to the Father through Jesus. The writer to the Hebrews twice affirms this:

> Let us then approach God's throne of grace with confidence, so that we may receive mercy and find grace to help us in our time of need. (Hebrews 4:16)

> Therefore, brothers and sisters, since we have confidence to enter the Most Holy Place by the blood of Jesus, by a new and living way opened for us through the curtain, that is, His body (Hebrews 10:19-20)

So, although this book has concentrated on v10 of Ephesians 3, the two following verses necessitate at least a mention to strengthen the tenor of Paul's writing.

The viewpoint I want the reader to take away with them in closing this book, is that all we have considered on our journey, has already been secured for us by Jesus' work on the Cross. While this is still being worked out as we journey through our Christian lives, the church also continues on its pathway that has been determined. Nevertheless, it is a comfort to us that the ultimate victory in the spiritual battle, which we as the church are engaged in, has already been won.

It may not seem as such, because of the tactics the enemy employs to derail and detract us from accomplishing our goal, yet we can have the assurance that the Father's desire will prevail and Jesus will be united with His Bride at the time set by God!

Paul further directs the reader to the fact that all the Father has determined to do has been done through Jesus. When we read the opening verses of John's gospel this aspect is clearly borne out:

> In the beginning was the Word, and the Word was with God, and the Word was God. He was with God in the beginning. Through Him all things were made; without Him nothing was made that has been made. (John 1:1-3)

We know that the Word was Jesus and here John receives revelation through the Holy Spirit that God worked all things through His Son, Jesus. So, it is no surprise then to read Paul's affirmation that the plan of God for the church to reveal His wisdom has been completed through Jesus.

This is of tremendous importance for us as Christians, as it underpins everything we do in our walk with God. As we have mentioned above, Paul adds the direct access we have to the Father through Jesus. What a wonderful privilege we have and we should take full advantage of this.

This ready access to God the Father, was bought for us at tremendous cost, both to God as Father and to Jesus as the Son through all that He gave up for us. It ushered in the church, which as we have seen, is made up of diverse people from across the world and reaches into every people group, in every part of their society, every language and every race.

The church is on a journey that began with the pouring out of the Holy Spirit at Pentecost, and is yet to reach its fulfilment in which we wait almost with baited breath, to see how that will be revealed.

While we can read in scripture an approximate description of the end times with its tantalising suggestions, yet it is in the working out and the detail, that we eagerly await the full revelation.

The church marches on with Jesus as its head and whilst there is much to lament how she is viewed in today's society, yet we can be assured the church will have a glorious finale, bringing full focus and glory to Jesus the Son of the living God.

> "Look, He is coming with the clouds," and "every eye will see Him. (Revelation 1:7)

Wrapping Things Up!

In His final revealing in all His glory, as Jesus comes for His Bride, it will surpass any blockbuster film ever made by man or woman here on earth. It will be like nothing ever seen before and will be the culmination of all the struggles, heartaches, pain, suffering and advances the church has experienced through over two thousand years of her existence.

He who testifies to these things says, "Yes, I am coming soon."

Amen. Come, Lord Jesus.

(Revelation 22:20)

At the very heart of Christianity is relationship — our relationship with God and His great desire for relationship with us. In this book you will see how God determined to restore the broken relationship between us and Himself through Jesus Christ. **Discovery** leads you through the basics of Christianity and covers such questions as *'Who is God?'*, *'Who is Jesus?'*, *'What is the significance of the crucifixion and Resurrection'* and many others.

Discovery has been written with two groups of people in mind — first for those who have had no or very little experience of Christianity and are wanting to find out more about the Christian faith and second, for those who have recently become a Christian and want to begin finding out more about the commitment they have made to their newfound Christian faith.

To purchase your copy, contact info@discoverchristinity.co.uk

www.ingramcontent.com/pod-product-compliance
Lightning Source LLC
Chambersburg PA
CBHW041143110526
44590CB00027B/4106